THE GENTLE WILL

OTHER BOOKS BY GEORG KÜHLEWIND

Becoming Aware of the Logos: The Way of St. John the Evangelist

From Normal to Healthy: Paths to the Liberation of Consciousness

The Life of the Soul: Between Subconsciousness and Supraconsciousness

The Light of the "I": Guidelines for Meditation

The Logos-Structure of the World: Language As Model of Reality

Stages of Consciousness: Meditations on the Boundaries of the Soul

Star Children: Understanding Children Who Set Us Special Tasks and Challenges

Wilt Thou Be Made Whole?: Healing in the Gospels

Working with Anthroposophy: The Practice of Thinking

The Gentle
WILL

GUIDELINES FOR
CREATIVE CONSCIOUSNESS

From what is thought to Thinking,
From what is felt to Feeling,
From what is willed to Willing

Georg Kühlewind

Translated by Michael Lipson, Ph.D.

LINDISFARNE BOOKS
2011

2011

LINDISFARNE BOOKS

An imprint of Anthroposophic Press, Inc.

610 Main Street, Great Barrington, MA 01230

www.steinerbooks.org

Cover image: copyright © by Renars Jurkovskis (shutterstock.com)
Book design: William Jens Jensen
Cover concept: Mary Giddens

Translated by Michael Lipson from the German edition,
*Der sanfte Wille: Vom Gedachten zum Denken, vom Gefühlten zum Fühlen,
vom Gewollten zum Willen* (Freies Geistesleben, 2007)

Printed in the United States of America

LIBRARY OF CONGRESS CATALOGING-IN-PUBLICATION DATA

Kühlewind, Georg.
[Sanfte Wille. English]
The gentle will : meditative guidelines for creative consciousness : from what is
thought to thinking, from what is felt to feeling, from what is willed to willing /
Georg Kühlewind ; translated by Michael Lipson.
    p. cm.
Includes bibliographical references.
ISBN 978-1-58420-093-2
1. Spiritual life—Anthroposophy. 2. Meditation—Anthroposophy. 3. Will—
Religious aspects—Anthroposophy. I. Title.
BP596.S66K8513 2011
299'.935—dc22

2011005391

Contents

INTRODUCTION
THE STORY OF THIS BOOK

If you practice meditative exercises over a long period, over decades, you have an experience analogous to repeated readings of a demanding book. New discoveries, new aspects, new facets, shine forth at every turn. When that happens, you can feel guilty that the later discoveries could not be included in your earlier descriptions. Concerning the path of meditative practice (the path of knowledge, the inner path), I would like to remedy this lack in some respects.

To do so, I must repeat some of the basics of what I have already described in earlier works; this repetition will also save the reader the trouble of looking things up. The longer you practice these exercises, the more clearly you experience the movements of consciousness within them: they become transparent to the active attention that carries them out. First, the movements of thinking become apparent, then those of feeling, then the processes of willing. These three are always intertwined (will, for example, is always active during practice), but one of the three predominates. Feeling and willing grow *luminous* only when they begin to grow cognitive (knowing) as well. This happens when thinking dissolves into feeling, or when feeling, already cognitive, dissolves into willing.

My involvement with the forms of human willing began long ago, as can be seen from my essay "The Reversal of the Will" (*Goetheanum*, 2/9–86; see appendix), or from my chapter "The

Schooling of Attention" in *Practicing Freedom* (1988). In 1996, my friend Hartwig Volbehr asked how the *qi* exercises with which he had long been familiar could be understood in terms of inner processes (see the chapter "Exercises of the Will," exercise 36). This led to experimental and meditative research whose result, largely, is this book. For this impulse, and the joint work that we have engaged in since then, I would like to extend my heartfelt thanks to Dr. Volbehr.

To arrive at the luminous, cognitive experience of the will, we have to progress through the previous stages very intensively. The practitioner must experience living, pure thinking—that is, form-free thinking—which then passes over into a kind of feeling that has been prepared for in advance. Otherwise, though feeling may become light-filled and joyous, it will not be experienced as cognitive. Feeling must be pursued in a similar way to lead to cognitive will.

It has been a long journey, then, to investigate the "gentle will" in its origins. The results, however, can be helpful for those at the beginning of the cognitive path. Actually, every practice, every exercise of consciousness, is carried out with the gentle will. It is good to know this even if, initially, you cannot yet fully activate the gentle will. In the course of practice, it will begin to gleam with light.

What we call "the experience of the body" has revealed itself as the experience, the sensation, of a *husk* of sensations that "surrounds" the body (non-spatially, but we are forced to use spatial images). At the same time, the whole meaning of "body practices," such as concentration on the breath, has revealed itself as the evocation, the bringing-to-consciousness, of the subject who undertakes the exercises. This is the one who observes, who experiences them—and who cannot be the body or the sensation itself, for these are the *objects* that the subject experiences. Actually, any object (not just the body) could serve this purpose: to point toward the subject.

In everyday life, we generally understand and value the objects about us in terms of their usefulness, so that the subject is "forgotten" as being "unimportant." In consciousness practices, however, objects are selected regardless of their usefulness. They regain, instead, the original function of all objects: namely, to point toward the true subject.

The gentle will is free of "me-feeling," in contrast to the activities of the hard will. This hard will works through a shell of egoism, mostly through the sense of touch,[1] and for this very reason loses its effectiveness, in every sense, and grows muffled.

For the relatively brief span of the exercises, we operate in a style that would be the wished-for ideal in everyday activities as well. If you have experiences during the periods of practice, then the results attained in these brief periods gradually spread out to everyday life.

In our current civilization, everyday life is governed by the principle of usefulness, and so by the "hard will" of egoism. This has already brought the world to the brink of catastrophe, whatever technocrats may say or think about it. I see no other hope of

---

1. The sense of touch is included in every bodily act, and transmits almost nothing beyond the sensation of the part of the body with which one has touched an object. One knows right away whether one has touched it with one's thumb or one's little finger. Other senses are not like this at all. For example, in seeing we do not feel our eyes. In touching, I initially learn almost nothing about what has been touched, other than that it is not I (i.e. not my body). Whether it is hard or rough I learn only by moving the part of the body that is touching, that is, only through the inclusion of the sense of movement and balance. But the sensory sheath or husk is always stimulated: *that* we experience.

avoiding destruction than for our mentality to change. This means for the hard will to become the gentle will. And this would be the *metanoesis* ("repentance," or literally, "change of sense") advocated by John the Baptist: giving new sense to human existence.

Practical Advice for the Reader

As with my previous books, this book is not simply to be read. Rather, its full "contents" develop only through a kind of doing. This is the reader's own doing: pondering, contemplating, meditating. In the text itself, you will find passages marked "Contemplation" and others marked "Contemplation/Meditation." The former are thoughts you can *ponder* over: deepen, continue, and extend them for yourself. The latter are meditative texts that can and should first be contemplated in this sense, but are then to be *meditated*.

Both processes are described in the chapters on meditation in many of my former books. The aim of all these books is to help the reader to move for brief periods from everyday thinking (past thinking, dialectical thinking, discursive thinking) into a higher level of thinking and understanding. Any other kind of knowing (knowing *about* this or that or a supposed understanding of the results of spiritual research through everyday thinking) is, in my view, simply a heap of obstacles, a dead weight—junk.

Georg Kühlewind
Budapest, 1999

FIRST PRELUDE

We live in a world of meanings, though we are convinced that we live in a world of things.

Yet every *thing* has meaning. Tell me a thing that doesn't have meaning! If you can name it, it is already not completely devoid of meaning. At first, we grasp meanings through thinking, or we try to. And sometimes we make new meanings.

But we don't know how we think.

We become conscious only of what has already been thought.

For the small child, for archaic peoples, for some angelic human beings[1] like St. Thomas Aquinas, reality consists of meanings. These meanings precede the individual things, both in human activity and, according to tradition, in divine activity. First comes the idea of the thing, then the thing. First the meaning, then the sign. This applies to thoughts, too, to the extent that they appear in signs.

Signs consist of configured matter: waves of air, ink, bodily gestures. Meanings are not made of matter. Therefore, understanding, too, proceeds immaterially. Matter-less meaning cannot be "understood" through material processes. The one within us who understands is also free of matter.

We read material signs for their matter-free meanings. Thinking, thoughts, thinkers, are matter-free.

---

1. For angelic beings, reality is only meanings; they have no awareness of touch-reality, which is the standard for most humans; such beings have nothing with which they could touch. In the case of Thomas of Aquinas, we find this experience explicitly stated. The truer a thing is, which means the more it expresses its being, its meaning, the realer it is. It is as if Thomas knew nothing of touch-reality—just like the angels.

The first goal is to experience thinking. Initially, that through which meanings are made, that through which meanings are understood—the thinker—remains hidden.

It is time to experience the light that makes everything visible, the light of meaning, the light of the Word.

From Thoughts to Thinking

Thoughts about Thinking

We do not know *how* we think—just as, when we speak, we are unaware of the activity of our own speech organs. We become conscious of the "already-thought" thought. How it comes about in the first place is hidden. There are two possible reasons. First, we are not conscious in the very process of thinking, and this would be reason enough for its "how" to stay in the dark. The other reason could be that we are so immersed in thinking, so identical with its process, that there is no one left to observe it.

Contemplation 1: We awaken to consciousness when thinking has already taken place and is in a state of rest: in the "already-thought."

Logic, as a science, attempts to formulate the laws, the how, of thinking, in retrospect. We already think logically without having studied logic, just as we can speak our mother tongue properly without any knowledge of grammar. Logic therefore must concern itself with logical forms, with movements of thinking, with a conceptual thinking, that has already appeared without benefit of "logic." Hence, logic can never be final or finished: for we can always produce new logical sequences.

Contemplation 2: First, there is logical thinking, then logic as a field of study. First there is language, then its explicit grammar.

That there is such a thing as the thinking *process* we can conclude from the fact that the previously thought continually increases and changes. We realize this because we have the capacity to reflect, so that we can direct our attention to thinking's past—to all that is past within our consciousness. This capacity is given to us without personal work, effort, or study.

We look at the past, "cooled-off" thinking from the *present*. Normally, we never experience the present itself, even though it is from this present that we look at both past and future. When we look at these, we lift them into the present—for a homeopathically brief instant. However, we become aware of them (even of images of the future) only when they are once again separated from the present, from the process of thinking and mental picturing. They stand before our inner sight as the "already-become"—for an awareness that looks at them from the present.

Contemplation 3: Only the present is reality.
(This is also a suitable theme for meditation.)

Presence of mind is a brief flash of two elements: spirit and presence, or intuition and presence—suddenly, and without preconsideration. We can ask, "What keeps us from *always* having presence of mind or, at least, from having it at will?"

We can reflect on this rare occurrence in retrospect. Something "occurs to us," for example, the solution to a dangerous situation. Moreover, we can sense that the solution "just *came*." We did not work it out; we didn't think about it (generally there is no time for that). Why does it happen only in situations of danger or extreme importance?

Observation shows that in the moment of danger we are fully concentrated. Attention is completely *in* the situation. Could it be that at least part of what prevents us from continual presence of mind is that our everyday attention is so distracted? Could it be that our thinking works along well-worn tracks, through fixed concepts, intermixed with other mental elements like wishes, prejudices, and preconceptions? In that case, there are two steps necessary for the elimination of our obstacles: the heightening our *capacity to concentrate* and the *purifying* of our thinking.

Contemplation/Meditation 4: What is "this" in contrast to "that"?

If we try to purify our thinking, we find that this purification and concentration point toward the same goal. By thinking about thinking, as enlightening as it may be, we remain on the same level of everyday consciousness. We simply multiply the objects of thinking, without changing their quality.

Such a change, as with every *capacity*, comes about only through *practice*, through exercise.

FIRST GROUP OF EXERCISES: PURIFICATION OF THINKING AND MENTAL PICTURES

Traditionally, "purification" was the first step in the development of heightened capacities for cognition. Since in our time thinking/mental picturing is the soul's only autonomous capacity, the path of schooling begins for us with the purification of these functions.

Exercise 1

We take a simple theme to think about and to picture mentally: for example, what we plan to do today or tomorrow, or what we did yesterday, or what the next step should be in our child's education, or what the next step is in the solution of a problem, and so forth. It should not be an entertaining, seductively interesting theme.

We begin to think about it, to make mental pictures of it, and attempt to avoid the associations that lead away from the line or from the network of the theme. In other words, we try to think continuously and to stay with the theme, avoiding jerks and interruptions. We try to notice any accompanying feelings, and do not allow them to influence the activity of thinking and making mental pictures. The process should proceed as objectively as possible. Accompanying nuances of feeling should be noticed, but should not compromise the process of thinking. This exercise can last five to ten minutes.

Once it is over, we look back on the course of thought and note how we deviated from it: the interruptions, the feelings that came up. We also note when or where they appeared during the whole inwardly experienced course of the exercise.

Exercise 2

We repeat Exercise 1, but now with a theme that is very interesting and attractive to us. Afterward, we compare 1 and 2, paying attention to the differences in the number and intensity of our distractions, to the quality and intensity of our feelings. The goal of both exercises is to maintain the continuity of the thinking process.

Exercise 3

The second step in the purification of thinking consists in avoiding all perceptual elements. For there is an element of materiality in every sensory perception, and this element is impenetrable to thinking. Where thinking/mental picturing bumps up against matter, it bounces off. Apart from its *qualities,* matter is unthinkable. Thinking only touches against it, as if from outside.[2]

Contemplation/Meditation 5 : Matter is unthinkable.

The exercise consists in choosing a theme for thinking that contains no perceptual elements. For example, choose a sentence from the prelude: "We don't know how we think," or a sentence from one of the first Contemplations, or a mathematical, philosophical, or logical truth or law. We try to think these "abstract" sentences further, avoiding mental pictures. The more we do so in a concentrated way (that is, the more continuously we do so), the more transparent the process becomes for thinking. After this exercise, we compare the experience of the first three exercises.

Exercise 4

We attempt to grasp (that is, to understand) the meaning of connective words like *yes, no, but, or, indeed, nevertheless, and, so, how, as, whether, if, otherwise, without,* and so forth. We do not want definitions or explanations of these words through *other* words. We do

---

2. We do not know the ideas, the concepts, of natural objects. We only have names for them. These designate an appearance, not a function. We have no understanding of their function in the way we do for fabricated objects. We understand "chair," not according to external characteristics, but according to its function. The appearance can vary greatly. In the case of "oak," we do not know the function; we stick to the form of the leaves, of the branches, of the bark, and so forth. We *recognize* it, but we do not *cognize* it. We experience the specific quality of substances (silver, glass, water) and experience something generic about them (spatiality, mass, weight). Chemistry is occupied with the quality; physics with the common characteristics of substances. Neither the quality nor the common characteristics are *understandable* for us, since we do not know their function. We define the corresponding concepts and operate on them mathematically wherever possible, without being able to penetrate them. Fabricated things, too, we understand only up to the point of their physical substance.

not want to say, for example, that *yes* means *assent*. We seek only the inner gesture of understanding. These words involve no perceptual elements. They are the articulation points, the joints, of speech. They are inner gesture and nothing else. It is instructive to compare the corresponding expressions in other languages (*but* = *aber*), and to be aware of differences in meaning.

Contemplation 6: The meanings of all these connective words are not to be found in the perceptual world. Where do they come from? What is their role?

Exercise 5

We try to grasp the meaning of adjectives, like *good, beautiful, big, little, long, slow, dark, round, angular,* and so forth. We can realize that these words can indeed relate to perception, though not necessarily (think of a "big" idea). Yet they, too, do not originate in the perceptual world. To see something as triangular, for example, you have to have previously the concepts of *three* and *angle*. Numbers are perhaps the best examples of the relationship between what is grasped in thought and what is grasped through the senses.

Exercise 6

We try to express the sentences in Exercise 3 in different words. Then, if possible, we translate the sentences into a foreign language. We can try this exercise with the sentence just before this one: "We try to express"; or with this very sentence: "We can try this exercise."

Contemplation 7: What is it that we translate?

Thoughts about Language...
Words, Sentences, Concepts, Presence, and Understanding

Contemplation 7 can show us that the meaning of a sentence being translated (and we do translate the meaning, not the words) can exist, at least for moments, without words and outside of any language—in the passage from one language to the other. This may be less surprising if we take into account the following Contemplation.

> *Contemplation 8: If we put something into a sentence, whether out loud or inwardly, how do we know what word to begin with, what word should come second, and so forth? How do we know which grammatical form to use? At times, you can find yourself deciding the language into which to translate it. It is not uncommon to be dissatisfied with the way we have expressed something. What is it we compare with the unsatisfactory expression?*

Pursuing these questions, it becomes obvious that the meaning or the sense of the sentence must already "be there" before I can choose the language, the words—that is, the signs—for the meaning. It is also well known that understanding a text goes beyond the understanding of the words. It can happen that we understand all the words of a sentence, but not the sentence itself. Or, just the reverse; we can fail to understand some of the words in a sentence, while we do understand the sentence as a whole; and that whole sheds light on the words not understood. This happens often in dealing with foreign languages.

The meaning or sense is present wordlessly, super-linguistically, before its appearance in signs. To understand it, the "understander" regains the spiritual form of the meaning. Even when we translate a single word, or replace one word with another in a given language, it is clear that we can separate the meaning from the sign or from the sound, and that the meaning exists independently of these sense-perceptible appearances. The next stage in the purification of thinking would be to think uninterruptedly, without words. This, and more, does in fact take place during moments of *presence of mind,* as if thinking took place with infinite speed, not step by step in time. For most adults today, to think intentionally, wordlessly, and without interruption, requires prior exercise. Exercise, however, can indeed bring it about.

Contemplation/Meditation 9: Words come from the wordless.

Behind words there stand "conceptualities:" a word is a sign for an understanding. You can also use words without really, fully understanding them in their essence (which is by no means rare), but even then we understand the word to mean *something.* Thinking in words really means thinking in concepts. The conceptuality of the words given in specific languages (not those in technical and scientific use) is never unambiguous. They can be used very flexibly, and can express new concepts.[1]

We can also designate *new* concepts using *old* words. This shows that concepts can exist even without words. The first concepts of a small child are given through the mother tongue; later, thinking emancipates itself from language and can arrive at new concepts.

---

1. For example, the Latin word *focus* meant the hearth or the fire in the hearth. Kepler used the word to mean "focal point" in its modern sense.

All this shows that human beings can think conceptually, yet without words. Generally, we think in finished, received concepts (not new ones), whether or not we are thinking wordlessly. Thus, the next step in the purification of thinking is to think without such fixed concepts.

Most concepts in the adult's repertoire are of the received, linguistically determined kind. These concepts, too, must be attained in the course of a life; that is, they must be *understood,* just as much as those relatively rare concepts that one has found on one's own. *Understanding* (the actual *forming* of concepts) occurs through a kind of thinking that does not itself proceed by means of concepts.

In early childhood, it is this kind of concept forming in thinking that predominates and through which the child understands the concepts that are given to it. To do so, the understanding, which is itself a continuum, must come to a halt. Where the process comes to a (temporary) halt, a concept arises. In adulthood, it is almost the reverse. Thinking takes place by means of already familiar concepts, between which there exist one or several gaps; just there, a new understanding arises and a new concept is formed.

An example of concept formation: We show a three- to five-year-old child objects that are circular, triangular, rectangular— and also others that have no familiar, named shapes. We show the child these objects in various sizes, colors, and materials. Until children have formed the concepts of circle, triangle, square, and colors, they cannot sort objects according to these characteristics. Concept formation occurs through selective attention. To grasp the concept of circle, for example, you have to disregard all the other qualities of the object, such as size, material, weight, color, and so forth, and direct your attention only to "that" one quality, the form. In the same way, attention must narrow itself down to form the concept of color, since a color never appears in isolation. Concept formation is always a narrowing of the stream of attentiveness. The history of words in every language demonstrates that in earlier times words designated greater, more comprehensive concepts; and the earlier we look, the broader the concept.[2]

Contemplation 10 : Is the shrinking of our concepts irreversible? Can concepts also increase in their content?

We have spoken here about a change in the conceptual life, and not about a change in the meaning of words, which is much easier to document historically. Yet this change in word meanings is only partially identical with the shrinking and simultaneous sharpening of concepts.[3]

If we consider the phenomenon of understanding, we find two striking traits: it happens with lightning rapidity, and it cannot be repeated. We cannot think the same thing twice; either the first understanding is completely forgotten, or we understand something new or different at the second attempt.

The speed of understanding has to do with its immediacy and its unmediated quality. Understanding may be prepared for long in advance; it can even take place step by step. Still, the act itself

---

2. For example, the Greek word *thymos* meant: breath, life force, the soul's power of spiritual activity, sensibility, heart, feeling, orientation, attitude, way of thinking, drive, desire, lust, tendency, decision, courage, passion, anger, reluctance. But it signified *as* one these meanings that appear listed separately in our dictionaries. Today, the original, huge meaning is split into many concepts.

3. Examples for the horizontal shift of meaning: in seventeenth century English, *subjective* meant something that belongs to the essence of the thing, to reality; in the nineteenth century, it became the expression for something that exists only in consciousness, without reality

(at each step) is, finally, instantaneous—as with every kind of finding. You can *look* for a long time, but you cannot *find* for a long time. Nor can understanding be analyzed, because it is itself the basis of all analysis, and of every kind of thinking. The real and *purest* thinking is understanding. Normally, it is brief (hence, too, the non-continuity of our thinking), and is accompanied by an unusual feeling of happiness or contentment: a process of leaps and bounds.

Contemplation/Meditation 11:
In understanding, we touch our heavens.

What becomes conscious from any act of understanding (apart from the "inkling," the aura of guessing that precedes it) is the result: the "already-thought." Even then, it becomes completely conscious only through its expression in words, which may not be rapid. It takes more or less time for the *understood* to emerge from the lightning, by which time it is already the past. Yet, obviously, understanding happens in the present. Such "presence" has two meanings: first, that understanding takes place neither in the past nor in the future; second, that we ourselves are present in the act. We know this because of a fleeting sense within the act of understanding, which we realize in retrospect without generally taking notice of it—the sense that it is *our* experience.

We can perceive a subtle difference between the experience of real understanding and, for example, the experience of *information*, for which no unique, intuitive understanding takes place (as in "Tomorrow it will probably rain.")

Contemplation 12:
We attempt to describe the difference just mentioned.

That we do *not* experience the present as such relates to both of the two characteristics of understanding: that it passes with lightning speed; and that we are present in the lightning—identical with it—whereas our normal experiences always take place dualistically, in the interval between subject and object—or so it seems. It could also be the case that for a brief instant (just as in the act of understanding) we are identical during every experience with just that which (a bit *later*) becomes the "experience-we-have-had." However, this question can be decided only by experiment, by the experience of identity and presence. Our goal then, is to move from thoughts to thinking or from the mental picture to the act of mental picturing. We can see that the purest thinking is understanding. Nevertheless, we cannot will this with our normal will; we must let it happen, let it occur to us. How do we do that? The goal would be to *lengthen* the instant of presence of mind, or understanding, and have the experience in *that* way, rather than in retrospect.

*Contemplation 13: What is the relationship
between presence of mind and understanding?*

Theoretically, pure thinking (the purest thinking) is a continuous, wordless, unbroken understanding beyond language and beyond concepts: the thinking of genius. We cannot produce it at will, and are happy if we touch into it at moments. In the brief moments of presence of mind, of understanding, we can notice complete, exclusive concentration and, at the same time, self-forgetfulness? Could the practice of these elements be a pathway to our goal?

PATHWAYS TO THE EXPERIENCE OF PRESENCE

Apart from those rare instants of presence of mind, when are we concentrated and self-forgetful? We are concentrated when we have to be; when there is a reason to be; when we want to solve a problem; or when something is very attractive, aesthetically or otherwise. These are all external occasions that have a certain effect on us in the context of our lives and that activate our will. How would it be (and what could we achieve) if we could produce a concentrated state by ourselves, without external reasons and motivations—that is, out of freedom? Then it would be completely *our doing;* and, because it would take place without a goal, the attentional will, having no other aim, could experience itself far more.

"Our own doing" means that the theme for attention should not be given through other processes, is not a percept, but is instead a mental picture or a thought (which cannot be given from without but must be produced by attention itself), whether a memory, a fantasy, or thinking. In this case, attention is concentrating on its own creation. We call it "active attention." In it, we can sense the possibility of attention meeting itself—that is, experiencing itself in its activity, rather than where it has already become an object, an image, a thought, a thing. The theme should be neither attractive nor repulsive. If the theme is attractive, then it requires no inner exercise of strength to stay with it. In addition, the theme should be understandable for the practitioner; that is, it is conceptually transparent. This criterion is met by fabricated objects. In the "Meditation" chapter, we will discuss how to proceed beyond fabricated objects, to thoughts and symbols.

Exercise 7

We choose a simple, familiar object (such as a button, needle, pencil, or ring); look at it carefully if need be; then put it aside, or close our eyes, and try to picture the object. This goes better the more we simply "let the picture come," as we do in memory (when we "call yesterday afternoon to mind," we do not have to *piece* the image together). It is as if we inwardly asked the question, "How does the object (needle, spoon) look?"

First, we let the image come up briefly; on the second or third attempt, we try to have it linger. We accompany the image of the object with thoughts, describing its shape, its qualities, what it is made of, and so forth. Then, we try to picture it in its function (the spoon "spooning"). Finally, if the previous attempts ("stages" which merge into one another continuously) have gone well and without distraction, we try to concentrate on the idea of the object, which the inventor had before his or her inner eye: the function, before any material object embodied it.[4] The duration of this exercise should be about three to five minutes (after overcoming any initial problems).

The mental picture alone can already yield the following experiences. The first is that it is not sufficient for the image to appear *once* if we want it to linger longer. It all too easily disappears right away, and consciousness becomes occupied with other, associated contents. If we want to hold onto the image, we have to produce it continually; it has to be nourished continually by a *stream* of attentiveness. In this case, "letting it come" means an ongoing process of letting it arise, out of a gentle, light, playful stream of

---

4. Instructions for the concentration exercise are in Kühlewind, *From Normal to Healthy*, chapter 5.

attentiveness—not cramped or cramping, not "hard will." This stream flows into the picture, which thereby arises and lingers. At first, we content ourselves with the image that we are able to hold for a few minutes. After each exercise, we look back at how it went.

We may notice, through this process, that (apart from distractions) it is only the image, or mental picture, that appears in consciousness, not the stream of attentiveness itself.

Discussion of Exercise 7

We can represent the process of concentration schematically as follows:

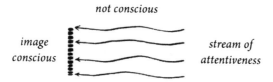

We direct attention quite consciously toward the image, but the movement, the "streaming-into-the-picture" remains outside our awareness; we do not experience how the image comes about, only the difficulty of keeping it there.

If, however, the stream of attentiveness grows more intensive, then changes begin to arise both in the image and in the "doing"— the production and sustenance of the image. The image becomes livelier, more powerful, and the activity comes to be felt as more and more *real*. You have the impression that someone is doing something, in a way that did not appear at the very start of the practice.

If we can stabilize these changes in practice, that is, if they are present in every exercise, then we can take a further step. We look at the object again, this time with a *global* regard, in the same way that we look at a human face without bothering about the details (the form of the nose or chin, and so forth). After all, we generally cannot recall these individual traits, though this does not prevent us from recognizing a face, or even imagining it, because we have a more global, "feeling" impression of it. Therefore, we try to look at the object with this kind of gaze. This attempt normally leads to an even livelier image, and we can notice that the movement of attentiveness acquires a subtle nuance of feeling.

Exercise 8

If attentiveness grows still further, then we can experience further changes in the course of practice. The image grows ever more luminous, in proportion to our *letting* it happen. It becomes "bigger," and moves closer to us. All these descriptions are forms of expression that do not reproduce the experience exactly, but simply indicate the direction in which the changes seem to go. In the experience itself, the practitioner will recognize what is valid in these descriptive attempts, and realize what they refer to.

One has the sensation that the image and the practitioner move closer and closer together, until they coincide completely; that is, one experiences oneself as *identical* with the image. The image, in this experience, is by no means simply static any more. What you are experiencing as identity is not a spoon but "spoon*ing*," not a cup but "cupp*ing*"—a verb, a functioning. At first, this dynamic may be felt as alienating. If you pursue the path of exercise, what you experience as identity becomes clearer and clearer. At this degree of concentration, you lose words and concepts. You let them fall away. What remains is a pure "*that*," a movement that could lead to the idea. You feel identical with this movement of the thinking/mental picturing attentiveness, with the original idea, the essence of the object. You become its creative understanding. You have arrived at pure thinking/mental picturing.

Discussion of Exercise 8

The experience described above bears a similarity to experiences in the theater or at a concert, where we participate self-forgetfully in what happens on the stage or in the music, to the point where the fiction moves us personally (*is* it a fiction?). In exercises of consciousness, however, the aesthetic appeal, the aspect offered from without, is lacking; *we* have to do it all by ourselves. Just here lies the strength of the exercise, which leads to the next step that can hardly ever come about in aesthetic experience. In the background of this experience of identity, there is the fact that attention is our soul-spiritual essence.[5] It is just for this reason that we normally do not experience attention: we are identical with it. We become conscious of it only where attention becomes a form—its object at any given moment. If attention grows unusually intense, the identity with the object emerges into consciousness. This is even truer when the object itself consists of attentiveness, as in an image or thought (active attention), and nothing is given from without.

Exercise 9

Attention can increase in intensity without limits. If it increases beyond the point at which one has the experience of identity, it reaches a further stage. Here, we again become the stream of attentiveness that flows into the "image," but we now experience it *before* the "image," where it has not yet been "formed." As described above, the image becomes the living sign for a living meaning (called the "originary" idea), a sign inseparable from its meaning.

5. Kühlewind, *Aufmerksamkeit und Hingabe,* chapter 4.

The only other place this kind of sign occurs is for small children in the course of learning to speak, or for archaic consciousness, in which thinking and speaking, not yet separated, are identical. "*Before* the image" here means neither a spatial nor a temporal precedence, since the whole process plays out in presence. Still, as attentiveness moves into its configuration as the image, it is experienced in its still form-free state; that is, it experiences itself, and so becomes self, a self-aware I. This experience can be called "I AM."

Here, thinking/mental picturing is experienced in its purest, concept-free, image-free (pre-image) movement—that is, in its concept-forming, form-forming movement. This was the principal aim of this sequence of exercises. At the same time, and not separated from this movement, the practitioner attains the I AM, the first possible purely spiritual experience (at least for a moment), which flashes forth like an understanding. Only through the experience of our own presence can we know Presence—the eternal Now—and the presence of all other beings. Our schematic representation now takes the following form:

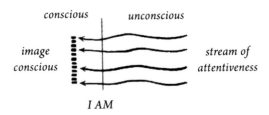

This experience is the same as the birth of the "true witness," as it is called in the New Testament.[6] This is the birth of the human being who is not automatically intermixed with the functions of the soul (with thinking, emotions, and impulses of will), but who instead,

---

6. The Gospel of John 5:31, 32; 8:13; 19:35; 21:4; III John 12.

looking on these functions—or at least at thinking—can make use of them. This "I AM" or Self is the experience of one's own spiritual being; therefore, it is also independent of success, failure, recognition, rejection, the opinion of others—and is equipped to handle stormy emotions. Instead of the storm of emotionality, an *aware*, cognitive feeling begins to awaken, and to play a growing role in one's life. The presence of this being as a momentary flash—real self-knowledge—is called Self-Consciousness Soul in Anthroposophy. If it lasts, it is called Spirit Self.

In this way, through exercises of thinking and mental picturing, we make two basic changes. One has to do with the inner life. In the experience of "it thinks," we develop an I AM or Self that not only is no longer entwined in thinking/mental picturing, but that can also direct this thinking power (which does not belong to it). The witness takes it in charge.

The other change has to do with the themes of concentration when these are simple, fabricated, utilitarian objects which we make use of as exercise-themes rather than for their everyday use. These objects become meaningful. We could say that they attain a new dignity, a new sacredness, by leading the practitioner's thinking through the course of their function and their "originary" idea. In this way, they are assimilated into the meaning-making activity of the exercise itself.

Our image of the world also changes dramatically with this experience. Everything in the world is experienced as a *becoming*, as a process or happening. Nothing "is," statically, any more. This is the world of the small child at a certain age (hard though the age is to specify), as well as that of archaic cultures, in which people also experienced everything as a happening—whether it was a rock or a mountain.

Only now does one know from experience what it means to say, "It thinks in me," which is also, after all, the secret of good, everyday thinking, too. We let it happen, and we limit ourselves to a gentle gesture of directing its course, as a shepherd guides the sheep that wander off to left and right back into the direction of the herd. When I experience, "It thinks," I am a present witness, not intermixed with the soul function of thinking, which is a spiritual being.

Actually, the sequence of exercises portrayed here extends our capacity to reflect. The given kind of reflection can orient itself only toward the past of thinking/mental picturing; now we can add the experience of presence.

Through this fundamental experience, consciousness approaches the otherwise supraconscious power that orients thinking and holds it within the bounds of logicality, which is a cognitive kind of feeling, the feeling of logicality, of evidence, of understanding or not understanding. The path to cognitive feeling has its start here. It can also dawn on the practitioner in a preliminary form that behind our allowing thinking to happen, there is hidden a supraconscious thinking will, a will that does not know in advance what it wills, an improvising will.

Contemplation/Meditation 14: The true witness does not witness in retrospect.

SECOND PRELUDE

We do not know how we think, because normally we do not experience the feeling that guides thinking.

We feel this feeling in its effects, not from within, only from without. The feeling that leads thinking and that lies hidden in perceiving stays behind the clouds of our inner sky.

If cognitive feeling goes unused, if it is not applied consciously, then it descends mostly into non-cognitive, meaningless forms. The first of these forms is the "me-feeling." On this base, further habitual forms are added. These are initially irreversible, since the true "I" does not enter into them.

Formed feelings (that is, emotions) hinder cognition and the inclusion of feeling in cognition. These forms have no meaning. They are noncommunicative; they bear no message. They can be dissolved in the course of exercises or (rarely) in the course of life, and become form-free capacities of feeling. In this way, we begin to experience feeling from within, in a feeling understanding.

A feeling (not an emotion) is just as understandable for feeling as a thought is for thinking. But understanding in feeling is an experience, while the understanding of a thought only *becomes* an experience when we dissolve the words, penetrate them, and in this way experience what they hide—the experience to which they point. We would have to go through them, dissolve them. *They dissolve into feeling.*

From Thinking to Feeling

Thoughts and Feelings—Thinking and Feeling

Exercises of thinking are possible because thinking/mental picturing is autonomous. We can think whatever we want to think or mentally picture, at least for a while, as long as associations do not compromise this autonomy, and as long as consciousness doesn't waver from its intention. What we have described as the purification or concentration of thinking can also be formulated as a striving for continuity. The continuity of thinking is interrupted by elements that arise that are not elements of thinking, but associations or perceptual elements ("unreadable" for thinking, not transparent), or through words and concepts, which act as stopping points in the continuity of understanding. Through the gradual elimination of these elements in concentrating, we arrive at pure thinking, at the concept-forming movement of thought that we strive to maintain in its flowing.

When we compare these processes with feeling, the first difference is that we have no autonomy in feeling; we cannot feel what we want to feel, at will. We cannot choose one from the palette of feelings and have it fill our consciousness in the same way that we choose an image or thoughts in the concentration exercise. When we feel something, it is usually an outer circumstance, a mental picture, or a bodily process that releases the feeling. We cannot make something new in the realm of feeling in the same way that is possible in the field of thinking.

The goal of the exercises of feeling is to develop a "cognitive feeling." Normally, by "feeling" we mean emotions: noncognitive waves of feeling that overwhelm us (anger, jealousy, envy, depression, and so forth). We can partially control the appearance of emotions in our behavior, but we cannot determine whether they are present or absent in us. Cognitive feelings come up only at the edges of our feeling life, in relation to artistic experiences, or in our professional life (therapists, teachers), if all goes well.

Behind thinking, then, we have discovered the feeling of logicality as the power that orients thinking. If we are to exercise cognitive feeling, we cannot skip the stage of pure thinking; cognitive feeling can be developed consciously only on this basis. This principle does not relate to aesthetic feeling, which is another story, and to which we will return.

The origin of thinking lies in cognitive feeling. We can guess as much from the feeling that something is *evident*, from the feeling for what is logical. It is confirmed by observation of young children and by the study of archaic cultures. It is through cognitive feeling that the small child receives the meaning of the first few hundred words, as well as grammatical forms.[1] The technical, medical, and architectural feats of archaic peoples (undertaken without analytical knowledge based on thinking) indicate the presence of a lost capacity to interact successfully with what nature gives us.

The more continuous thinking becomes, the more it turns into cognitive feeling from which it originates. It dissolves into feeling, becomes "global" (remember the global glance with which we look at a face), less sharp and analytical, but even more inclusive. The path to cognitive feeling leads through concentrated, pure

---

1. Kühlewind, *Der Sprechende Mensch,* chapter 3.

thinking. This is the original feeling, both for the individual and in the history of consciousness.

When and how was this feeling lost? The answer can be observed, again, both in children and in the history of culture. When children, when the people in a culture, begin to speak in the first person (to say, *I, me, mine*) with regard to the body, with which they have identified themselves, then a new feeling emerges that is noncognitive: the "me-feeling." The use of first-person pronouns is the sign of this identification and of the development of the me-feeling. This me-feeling covers the body like a feeling-coat, without actually cognizing the body.[2] The transformation of cognitive feeling into noncognitive feeling begins here, and the result is what we call emotions: feeling-forms of a noncognitive character. The path of exercise in regard to feeling consists in our attempting to liberate the feeling forces that have been trapped and formed in emotions. We try to make them form-free again, and so capable of cognition.

Contemplation 15:
Only form-free forces can cognize forms, or make forms.

Emotions run along a polarity that stretches from *"good"* to *"not-good"*—that is, *"good for me"* to *"bad for me."* Emotions are egotistically hued, and heighten the me-feeling, even those that seem to be unwanted, such as anger, hate or sadness. We enjoy them in a way; otherwise, we would not exaggerate them.[3] The cognitive, feeling forces are essentially objective, like thinking, which in principle lives on the far side of this *"good for me"*–*"bad for me"* continuum. Truth is neutral about our wishes.

2. Kühlewind, *Aufmerksamkeit und Hingabe,* chapter 7.
3. Kühlewind, *From Normal to Healthy,* chapter 4.

*Contemplation 16: We look for a feeling experience
that belongs to neither end of this polarity.*

It is almost impossible to name the experiences of cognitive feeling.
Poets strive to do so in various ways; there are no socially accepted
names for these feelings. Emotions, too, have a scant nomencla-
ture. There are, for example, as many nuances of anger as there are
innumerable, individually differentiated trees that are all called
"beeches." We are unaccustomed to distinguish between nuances
of emotion. Exercises in this area must therefore take place wordlessly, for the most part. Still, finding and sensing differences forms
the initial basis of practice.

What we call a "concept" or an "idea" in the realm of thinking
can be called a "feeling form" or a "feeling idea" in the realm of
feeling—analogous to the expressions "a musical idea," or "a paint-
erly idea."

EXERCISES IN COGNITIVE FEELING

Exercise 10

We recall emotions we have experienced that "have the same
name": for example, different angers, or different people with
whom we have been angry. We try to *sense* differences between
these cases; differences not only in strength, but above all in quality. After all, we are not angry in the same style, with the same
"color," in different cases. It is not important to describe or name
these differences. We can designate them with the names of the
people involved, or of the place or time, or give them any arbitrary
name. We then take another kind of emotion from memory, for
example, envy; and compare two or three such experiences in

terms of their "taste." Then we turn back to the first kind (anger). Once again, we turn to the second kind (envy), then back again, alternating. In the first such alternations, the differences in quality are usually clearer, more palpable. They can even increase in distinctness with further repetitions. We perform this exercise until the experiences of quality remain stable. In the next days, we try again. The differentiation will increase.

Exercise 11

We try to experience the differences between two cognitive feelings. They can be aesthetic feelings; we can choose as themes two poems, two novels, two pieces of music, pictures, and so forth. We can compare two styles of literature, of music, and so forth. We can also compare two truths if we *feel* them as truths. We proceed in the same way as in Exercise 10.

Exercise 12

Those involved in mathematics, natural science, or logic, are familiar with the feeling of "*therefore*." A proof or a syllogism proceeds by means of so-called accepted or easily acceptable premises, such as "A implies B; B implies C; *therefore* (it follows that) A implies C" (which doesn't always follow naturally). "Therefore" refers to a feeling of evidence. We can, as an exercise, follow different sequences of proof and feel our way into this feeling of evidence, first in each individual case, then in comparing two or several cases.

Exercise 13

We take a feeling experience from Exercise 10 (an emotion) and compare it with a cognitive feeling from Exercise 11 or 12. This is a greater qualitative difference than in these two previous exercises, but both of these are necessary preliminaries for correct experience.

Parenthetical Remark

In these exercises, we are using the gentle will. We allow the memory of emotions and of cognitive feeling experiences to come up, and the more we do this in a relaxed fashion, the more often we repeat them, and let them return, the more lively they become. We prepare this return through mental pictures, memory pictures of how the emotions arose. The more lively the pictures, the more those feeling experiences will reemerge living and warm.

Exercise 14

Once again, we take an emotional scene from the past and we try to evaluate the strength of what we felt then, as well as to sense it qualitatively; that is, sense the specific anger, for example, in the former situation. When we have found this quality, we try to sense *in feeling* whether our inner and outer behavior at the time was appropriate to the situation and adequate to it, or whether it was exaggerated. Did we overdo it "a little bit" from hidden motives? Generally, we find that our reaction exceeded its cause.

Contemplation 17: What is the appropriate degree of reaction?

This contemplation can lead to surprising results.

Exercise 15

We can try to reduce our agitation during the memory of an emotion. We also notice that the agitation itself, even if its cause is quite impersonal ("it didn't happen to me") has a me-feeling, egotistical component, and what is exaggerated about it derives from this component. If exercises of thinking and mental picturing have preceded this exercise, or if they run in parallel with exercises of feeling, then the growing proximity of Self-experience (or Self-experience itself) helps in mastering emotional upheavals.

We repeat the diminution of emotion in various memories. Generally, little remains of the agitation that cannot be further minimized.

Exercise 16

The practitioner will certainly have noticed that in all these feeling exercises, a cognitive feeling is awakened and utilized. Now we make a more conscious use of it. We again evoke an emotional moment from the past into our feeling consciousness, reduce it as much as possible, and then we try to sense the quality of the remaining emotion and with a *concentrated* thinking, alert to its theme to the point of identity, we try to dive into this quality. If this exercise is well prepared from both sides (from that of thinking and of feeling), then we experience how the firmer movement of thinking, when it dips into the churning fluidity of emotion, dissolves into it, becoming a feeling that first colors the emotion, then turns it into a cognitive experience. This kind of cognition is very hard to put into words, nor should we try to do so at first (to protect the experience from distortion). Rather, we simply let the experience of "Aha!" come and go within feeling. With many repetitions, words will also come.

This exercise has many benefits. On the one hand, we learn that even a feeling is cognizable; that is, it can dissolve. This does not refer to the rational finding of a cause, or the acquisition of intellectual knowledge, but to the calming and transformation of emotions into lighter, more transparent, cognitive inner gestures. On the other hand, we learn how to deal with emotions, even if initially with those of the past. This prepares us for a different stance toward present emotions as well. We learn through experience that concentrated thinking can change, relatively easily, into feeling intelligence.

Exercise 17

Looking back to concentration in thinking and mental picturing, we try to heighten the intensity of attentiveness still further, beyond the I-experience (becoming a Self) already described. If attentiveness as a movement into the theme has awakened to itself "before" the image (or theme), then in this further heightening, attentiveness remains continually awake; that is, the I AM becomes lasting (becomes Spirit Self for the duration of the exercise), and shifts more and more from pure, living thinking into the coloration of feeling. This shift is a continuum; there are no "stages," no rungs or levels with gaps between them. The structure of language constrains us to talk of stages because we cannot portray a continuum in its seamless transition. This constraint imposed by language is the reason that, in traditional accounts and elsewhere, we read about the various (4, 7, 9, or 12) "stages of consciousness," or about innumerable "cosmic spheres" in regard to the spiritual world.

We can again represent the process schematically:

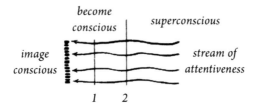

In the diagram, 1 and 2 refer to the first and second *named* experiences of the "I" (Spirit Self and Life Spirit, respectively). The "second" experience, compared with the first, is an earlier awakening (earlier with respect to the theme, though "earlier" here is to be understood neither temporally nor spatially). Experience 2 is a pure feeling, an intelligent feeling, with a Self that does not feel itself as an object (as in me-feeling). Instead, the Self experiences itself analogously to the purely thinking attentiveness in the first self-experience. Here, in the second experience, it is the feeling attentiveness into which pure thinking has dissolved.

For this Self, which can appear in the course of the exercise, the theme presents itself in nondualistic fashion. It becomes identity in the form of a specific feeling. We could perceive the whole world thus, if this kind of consciousness would only last. This is how the small child experiences the world at an early point in life (even earlier than when everything is experienced as process): as forms of feeling. Archaic cultures also had this kind of experience.

We can designate the second I AM experience, as well as the experiences between 1 and 2, as the perception of the *force* that moves the stream of attentiveness, and moves it in just such a way that it becomes the chosen theme. The force of movement in thinking/mental picturing is this feeling. If you want to draw or paint a picture, the pencil or brush has to be moved by the feeling of the theme; otherwise, the image is just patchwork. The stream of thinking, too, becomes alive only if it is carried by a cognitive feeling as its force of movement.

Exercise 18

If, in the concentration exercise, one has arrived several times at experiences 1 or 2, then one is only rarely overwhelmed with emotion. But even before this, after using the exercises with past emotional situations one can also attempt exercises with current, predictable emotions. If I know that I am likely to have a disturbing conversation in the near future, I can prepare for it. I do not prescribe a particular behavior, but attempt to prepare my concentratedness, precisely by concentrating on themes that have *nothing to do with* the conversation. If attentiveness is prepared, then I can undertake to enter intentionally into the emotion that is probably awaiting me, to approach it, as one may immerse oneself in the waves of the sea. I don't wait for the water to reach me, but actively go into it. The result can be that, while I fully experience the emotion, it does not overpower me, or at least not fully—my head stays above the water. I can also recall how I "saved" a portion of the emotional intensity during previous exercises related to past situations, and attempt to apply all the experiences of those exercises to current, present emotions. Here begins a phase of the path that takes place in everyday life.

Parenthetical Remark

When we think or mentally picture something in exercises of concentration, we are lifting a thought or a mental picture out of the past and, for a moment, into the present of consciousness, and it generally happens without difficulty. Difficulty arises when we want to *hold* the memory. Our being able to bring something from the past into the present shows that our essence, attentiveness, is present, without our directly experiencing it. Out of this supraconscious presence we have access to the past, to pictures, thoughts, and objects. Feelings, however, actually have no past; if we experience a feeling or an emotion, it is continuously present. This is why I cannot simply bring up an emotion into memory (that is, into presence) in the same way I can bring a thought or an object to which I direct my attentiveness. Instead, I have to use thinking/mental picturing to conjure up the situation in which I experienced the emotion. This can be very hard, or it may not succeed at all.

Contemplation / Meditation 18: Feelings are only now.

Exercise 19

We bring an index finger into an upright position and concentrate on it *as a sensation*. We let our thinking/mental picturing rest, and we try to feel the finger. We do not look at it, and we disregard everything we know anatomically or otherwise about the finger. We pay attention only to the sensations, for three to five minutes.

If we do this exercise correctly, in accordance with the indications given above, we notice that we do not experience the finger at all. We do not sense it globally or in its parts (bones, muscles, joints, skin, nerves), but only a sensation that surrounds the finger on all sides like a bandage. The edges of this covering are indistinct in space. They are vague. You can also have the sensation that the finger is much thicker than we knew, or much longer.

Contemplation 19: Sensation senses only sensation.

Exercise 20

What we experience in Exercise 18 can be extended gradually to the whole body. First, we take an arm, hanging freely, and then two arms. If the sensing attentiveness oscillates between them, we can help ourselves with the mental picture of a string or lathe that connects the two arms. Then we try, standing up, to begin with the two feet and to slowly allow the sensation to mount through the whole body. The sensation is noncognitive; it is only the "me-sensation," in which we have dwelt since early childhood, experienced in concentrated form.

> *Contemplation 20: What we call the sensation of the body is a covering of sensation that surrounds the body.*

In these exercises, we can experience the me-sensation intensively and in its pure form, as far as it relates to the body. There is also a purely mental me-sensation or me-feeling, such as envy, vanity, and so forth, to which we shall return.

With growing facility in these exercises, we can direct attention to the inside of the body as well. We arrive at the same result; here, too, we perceive no body parts, but only the covering sensation around them.

Parenthetical Remark

The point of all exercises that direct attention to the body is (and was originally) to make it clear to the practitioner that it is not the body that experiences the body, but a subject that is independent of the body. The degree to which this subject, the witness itself, is experienced in these exercises, always depends on the intensity of the attentiveness. The less developed the "egoity-covering," the more easily the Being who experiences can shine forth.

Exercise 21

With frequent repetition of the preceding two exercises, we gradually notice a second feeling, an *observing* feeling. It is logically clear that neither the body nor the sensations we experience can be the subject of these experiences; yet the real subject generally remains hidden behind the object-oriented experience—behind all the objects. In traditional cultures, too, the point was to allow for the discovery of the experiencer of the body exercises (or exercises that included the body).

Through concentration on the body or on its parts, we can grasp the quality of the me-sensation quite precisely. Now we attempt to notice, at the very same time, the witnessing feeling, the sensation of the subject. Then we can compare the two sensations and work out the difference between them more and more in our *sensing*, without concepts and words.

Exercise 22

We perform a thinking/mental picturing exercise (as in Exercise 7), and pursue it as far as possible, at least to the point of identity: we become the theme. At the same time, we try to feel the quality of the experiencer *within* the exercise—that is, without losing the experience of identity. Afterward, we evoke an emotion from the past, immerse ourselves in it thoroughly, and try at the same time here, too, to experience the quality of the experiencer. If we succeed, we then compare the quality of the two subjects—in feeling, without concepts and words.

Exercise 23

One of the "Supplementary Exercises" recommended by Steiner ("supplementary," that is, to meditation) is *equanimity*. As in many other traditions, equanimity does not mean indifference or phlegmatic behavior, nor even that we avoid and suppress the outer expressions of emotional storms. The essence of this exercise is, rather, that we try to avoid exaggeration, and transform emotions partially into cognitive feeling. One tries not to be drawn into a storm of feeling automatically, as if through an irresistible stimulus; rather, one takes part in such situations with compassion, sympathy, and love. Cognitive feeling contributes soothingly, healingly. The goal is not cold nonparticipation, but a heightened capacity to feel.[4]

Exercise 24

Another of the so-called supplementary exercises is "freedom from prejudice." As with every exercise, this too can be deepened infinitely and is, in this sense, like the introduction to an inner gesture, to wonder. Freedom from prejudice does not mean simply becoming free from fixed ideas, deeply rooted opinions, wishful thinking, and everything else that can mislead everyday thinking. It also means that one prepares oneself for a new understanding. When confronted with something unknown, surprising, or unbelievable, our first impulse is to want to understand it with concepts already familiar to us. All too easily, the unfamiliar then finds its way into pigeonholes we have held ready long since. If we experienced the resurrection of someone who had died, would we accept it? Or would we right away have a sequence of thoughts

---

4. Kühlewind, *From Normal to Healthy,* chapter 5.

that "explained" it, reducing it to a natural process and letting its miraculous quality disappear?

The exercise can be very demanding insofar as the practitioner attempts, in meeting something unfamiliar, *not* to apply his ready-made conceptual net, but to refrain from doing so. In other words, the practitioner tries to keep his thinking quiet. This, in itself, is almost impossible, unless something else appears in place of conceptual thinking: the beginnings of a cognitive feeling. These beginnings are not a cognition, but only the untainted readiness to feel an empty feeling, in which, nonetheless, we can perceive the first sprouts of a feeling cognition as if in a dissolved form. We can see that this phase of practice presupposes a substantial mastery over the life of thinking and some preparation of the cognitive life of feeling.

In this sense, freedom from prejudice is "form-free" readiness. It is freedom from forms of thinking, feeling, and willing that come from the past. It is freedom from everything received, everything that has not dissolved into capacity. It is readiness, then, by the light of a new opening, to know something as completely new, at every level.

Parenthetical Remark

In a lecture cycle with the title *The World of the Senses and the World of the Spirit,*[5] Steiner shows how the reality of the created world can be experienced in the physical as "reigning will." Behind this, as its sense or meaning, we can experience "reigning wisdom." Both of these we know through a heightened cognitive capacity. But this means, above all, a heightened "I" or Self, aware of itself; other-

---

5. Steiner, *The World of the Senses and the World of the Spirit* (CW 134).

wise, the "higher cognition" would have no subject. This subject is not given; it has to develop itself from out of the givenness of the everyday "I" through exercises of consciousness. That is, it must release itself from its identity with the functions of the soul (thinking, feeling, willing), and become something like an observer of these functions. The path to this Self, and its cognitive fruits, have a decidedly *feeling* character, and reality too takes on a willing, feeling character. "Reigning" refers to the process-like nature of this reality.

Contemplation / Meditation 21: Reality is feelable.

The path portrayed here consists in four inner gestures, which lead by stages to our goal: Wonder; Reverence for Reality and Truth; Harmony with Cosmic Law (Cosmic Reality); and Assent to the World Process. The first three attitudes are *feeling*; the fourth emerges from feeling and touches into the sphere of willing. This path, given in this way, is for the practitioner who has gone through exercises of pure thinking and through exercises of feeling related to the past, and who has also begun to apply these in a current life situation.

Exercise 25

Wonder is the precondition for every original cognition: becoming free from past elements. This of course does not mean that past elements are superfluous, or that one simply forgets them, as if they were wiped from the slate. What plays the major role here is the process of dissolving experiences into capacities (which is also, by the way, the fundamental issue in every kind of teaching). Wonder cannot be evoked by a decision of the will; rather, we can merely remove the obstacles to wonder. The exercise of freedom from prejudice leads in this direction, as does the practice of inner calm. The latter, practiced intensively, is an inner silence, the cessation of the inner dialogue we conduct with ourselves incessantly; also it is the cessation of the shower of concepts with which we meet and swiftly judge everything that enters into our consciousness.

Freedom from prejudice is one exercise, and freedom from assumptions is the other exercise, that lead to the capacity for wonder. Even when we have learned to avoid the application of our store of concepts, we silently and unwittingly bring many assumptions along with us. One of these assumptions is that, just as we are right now, we can understand the phenomenon that is coming to meet us. Our whole past, our upbringing, our life circumstances, our life style, our cultural influences, all belong to these "assumptions," along with the language we live with. It is clear that the purification of thinking, if it goes deep enough, can also reconfigure these assumptions. Wonder is not there "once and for all," like a seed of understanding; rather it is like the good earth in which the seed can fall and sprout. We can stand in wonder before everything, if we have cleared away the obstacles mentioned here (and perhaps others that have collected in the course of our lives). The small child is still free from these hindrances; wonder comes naturally to children. Once wonder is reborn in an adult, he or she can also compare the various feeling-tones within wonder.

Exercise 26

Reverence or devotion for what presents itself to our thinking grows out of wonder as a natural attitude toward what is greater, toward what one does not understand and therefore cannot produce oneself. The new phenomenon is simply there, without my participation, and even *shows* itself. This is the nature of creation. It shows itself in order to be understood.

Contemplation/Meditation 22: Creation is unhidden.

As with wonder, almost everything is available for reverence. The essence of reverence (as in wonder and in the next two exercises) is to refrain from imposing our autonomous thinking. The virtue necessary for every higher cognition is prescribed here: that is, being able to wait. Waiting is not passivity, nor is it a foretaste or inkling; therefore, it is terribly difficult. It is simply a preparedness without aim, without anticipating a direction, merely the offering of a place for that which is to come.

Reverence, like the wonder from which it follows naturally, is not cognition, but preparation—a process of stepping *back* before what is to be cognized. We find the same movement backward in the next two states of the soul described by Steiner, but here too only in deep concentration, where attentiveness can experience itself further and further *before* the image or theme, moving backward toward its source.

Exercise 27

To place oneself in harmony with the cosmic law, as the third stance of the soul, is an adaptation (to use the term of St. Thomas Aquinas, *adaequatio*) in the direction of *becoming that*, of *becoming identical* with what one intends to cognize. We do not know what we are adapting ourselves to; rather, in Thomas's sense, the *adequatio* is mutual. What we are to cognize adapts itself to us, to our cognitive gesture, and we adapt ourselves, by means of this very gesture, to it. There is a mutual movement toward one another, because these two components of the world are related to one another.[6] What we then cognize is the result of the two movements. This adaptation is prepared in advance, in feeling, through harmony with the cosmic order.

Thinking is held back, so that things reveal themselves. They reveal themselves first to the gaze full of reverence. Then that "hearing" can begin by which the cognizer approaches the speaking of things. Harmony lets this speaking sound forth; it lets our feeling be influenced by "the things"—feeling which, in turn, can lead thinking to express what has been heard. The quality of the things activated by this soul stance is their "truth." In Thomas's sense (and in accordance with medieval and earlier linguistic usage) *truth* is the capacity of things to reveal their meaning, because they have a meaning. In fact, they *are* their meaning, which shines toward the prepared soul as the light of things.

> Contemplation/Meditation 23: *That things become real,*
> *is their light itself. (Thomas Aquinas)*

What we called "cosmic law" previously, is the light of things.

Exercise 28

Assent to the World Process is the name of the fourth stance of the soul. All four are necessary *before* thinking, as preparation, if thinking is to come into contact with reality. "Assent" means that the spirit/soul, the soul that cognizes, lets itself be imprinted by what shines toward it from the "thing" (which can also be something immaterial, a thought). Here, we should remember that the "thing" is a result of the mutual adaptation of cognizer and what is

---

6. Kühlewind, *Die Esoterik des Erkennens und Handelns,* chapter 4.

to be cognized. What allows itself to be imprinted can be called the reversed, receptive will.[7] It is with this will that the small child first approaches the world, and the adult tries to reproduce this imprintable will, but with consciousness of the "I." The person stands completely aside in assent, having done everything to let reality approach. You become indifferent as to whether it is you or someone else who receives the cognition, and even whether the cognition comes about at all.

Parenthetical Remark

The four conditions of soul described here have a common trait: the human being retreats before what approaches—does not grasp; learns to wait actively. This is the greatest degree of activity: holding back. This waiting is its own ripening, the letting go of the most deeply rooted "assumption" that, just as I am, I am able and worthy to understand everything, to cognize reality.

This holding back has two consequences. On the one hand, the (future) true "I" or Self draws out from its intermixture with the functions of the soul and becomes their "witness," their experiencer from within. (One cannot observe the soul's functions from "outside," but can only use them, for we are within them, without any separation). On the other hand, the intelligently feeling attentiveness, which is related to the four soul states, becomes gradually "emptier": it becomes objectless, but active. This is the general course of development; a capacity develops in the presence of objects, contents, so that then, freed from them, it can grasp and even create any object. Capacities are free from forms, though they deal with forms both receptively and productively.

---

7. See the second appendix of this volume, "Reversal of the Will and Encountering the Power of the Logos," page 93.

Contemplation/Meditation 24:
Capacities are form-free in their own area.

For this freedom, in order to be able to bear it, to be its subject, there has to be a Self at every level. Normal "capacities" are limited to an area (music, education, and so forth). What leads to the Self is the experience of the *general* capacity, the empty attentiveness from which, through limitation or selectivity, the individual, specific capacities arise.

The path portrayed here can also be characterized as one of purity of the soul functions. Purity means being free of forms, objects, contents, but also, above all, being free from the me-sensation that is the basis of egoism and the first object with which the human being becomes partially confused: the most inveterate "assumption."

For a human being who has realized empty feeling to the point of Assent in the Cosmic Process, and who has simultaneously realized the corresponding Self in empty, feeling attentiveness, the perceptual world reveals itself as changed. If we call this givenness which we perceive with the aid of our senses (not *through* them), the "sense world," then it is not this that changes. Rather, a meaning reality accompanies the sense perception, inseparable from it. When someone learns to read, it is not the letters, the imprints on the page, that have changed.

Third Prelude

We don't know how we think. This state of ignorance distorts all our knowledge.

We also don't know how we speak, how we move, how we will, what feeling is, who we are. We don't experience our attentiveness, through which we experience everything else. We don't know our own biography; otherwise, we would have no problems in life. We know nothing about our own destiny, nothing about the value of individual experiences, nothing about life and death, about the cosmos, about its beginning and end.

Whatever we do, do not do; think, do not think—everything is done with the will. What do we know about the will?

III.

From Feeling to Willing

Thoughts about the Will

When cognitive feeling begins to awaken, or has already awakened, the world that appears to this feeling gaze, to all sense domains, and to thinking, is altered. Everything appears as "feelable" will—both things and thinking. The things *want* to be the things that they are, and so it is with thoughts and even feelings. It is not the will *of* the things, the thoughts, the feelings; they *are* will and this will belongs, finally, like every will, *to someone.*

If we make something from given materials, our will is active in the process of shaping, forming, putting them together. Once the "thing" (which can also be a thought) is finished, then the formative "I," its will, separates from the finished thing and gives what has been shaped over to a lasting, preserving, reigning will, whose effect we mostly experience as "being," as if the thing, once made, possessed a "being."

Small children and archaic peoples directly experience the forming and preserving will in creation. We can at least have it in view, can think it.

Contemplation / Meditation 25: Everything is will.

Everything that has form (including thoughts and forms of feeling) is will. In perceiving (sensory or spiritual perceiving), we

46

experience this will for an instant. It radiates out to us from everything formed, and it imprints our attentiveness into what we perceive. We cannot will, with our will, *against* perception; if something is blue or rectangular, we cannot see it as red and round, no matter how hard we try.

Small children and archaic people experience the will of things because they experience them as meaningful, light-filled, feelable light to which they bring a reversed, imprintable will: "thy will be done" as my own will, and so they place themselves within the cosmic stream.

The adult of today cannot *will* this receptive will, cannot call it forth intentionally. We can experience it when we meet something greater than ourselves and open ourselves to it. This happens mostly in specific areas such as music, drama, science, and so forth. It was the same in archaic cultures; one person knew how to work with metals, another with plants, a third with illnesses. The priest-king, by contrast, was capable in many areas.

The receptive, primal will has a quality we can observe in small children. The child can reproduce whatever it receives. Generally, we call this phenomenon "imitation." It is in no way a conscious intention to imitate, however. A child can emit again what is imprinted into the receptive or reversed will. This is how a child "learns" to speak. On the one hand, children can reproduce the sounds, words, and sentences to the extent that they have heard those sounds, words, and sentences correctly. On the other hand, children experience in feeling the spoken intention of the speaker. They experience directly the meaning of what has been said, and so can "understand" the sense of the words and sentences and grammatical usages and apply them appropriately.

Adults preserve the imprintability of childhood, which extends to bodily imprintability in the areas of speaking and singing. We can reproduce at will, without practicing, and just as we have heard it, whether a given pitch or a previously unused, unheard of sound, or a word in a foreign language. The question we rarely ask is: How do the vocal chords, or speech organs, know how to reproduce what the ears have heard? We can answer this by referring to the imprintability of these bodily spheres; as soon as we hear something, the vocal chords and speech organs are silent participants. The case is similar for every capacity. Those who can absorb music with the cognitive, imprintable will can become composers. Those who can absorb it with feeling can become musicians.

In speaking, singing, or any artistic activity, there appears a special, double will. First, the conscious, attentive will is occupied with and directed toward the content of what is said, with the music, with the themes of the art. Second, the bodily will translates that content into the perceptual will in speaking, playing, and so forth. This second aspect is *supraconscious*. We do not know how we work our speech organs, how we move our hands and arms in an artistic activity, not even whether we learned such activities consciously. Once such activities become capacities, their activation shifts into the supraconscious.

This *expressive will* is the continuation of our childhood receptive (and simultaneously reproductive) will. In all the activities mentioned here, we can easily notice the receptive part, the formative inspiration. This is also the case in artistic speech, whereas in everyday life the content of speech can come from various uninspired sources. The movements of the speech organs by which it is accomplished remain supraconscious.

The supraconscious, double, expressive will described above is what we use in bodily expressive activities. Most bodily movements do not serve to express anything; instead, they serve a purpose. We can call it the work will or the useful will. It is with this that we move our body parts when we eat with a spoon, knife and fork, when we dig the weeds, drive our cars, and so forth. At first, we learn these movements consciously; later, they can be automatic. Still, we can distinguish these movements from expressive gestures through two traits: attention must stay with the bodily movements, at least somewhat, and the movements do not serve to express anything, to communicate anything. They carry no message.

Both forms of will have in common that we do not know how the bodily movement comes about. In the case of the work will we know the form of movement and, consciously, the movement. In the case of the expressive will, either we do not know the form of the movement (as in speaking) or we are not primarily interested in it (as in art). We are interested in the "message," which is lacking in the useful will (work will).

The expressive will, in contrast to the useful will, is not accompanied by me-feeling, and does not become automatic. Me-feeling arises during useful will through the sense of touch. The latter is also active during, for example, piano playing, but attentiveness there is only peripherally concerned with the fingers; it is directed primarily toward the music. Artistic movement is playful, not strenuous, and accompanied by an implicit witnessing in which the witness is not planning the movement.[1]

---

1. If we use the hard will in expressive bodily movements where the gentle will is appropriate, the movement becomes incomplete or wrong. When a pianist focuses on the fingers, the right touch becomes impossible, and the music is lost. In stuttering, the hard will is used to move the organs of speech;

There are acts of the will that do not result in bodily movement, or the resulting movement is only secondary, as, for example, thinking, remembering, understanding, guessing, learning, problem-solving. Evidently, one cannot "will" these activities with a goal-oriented will; one *lets them happen*. One allows thinking to move under one's light, careful guidance; one allows memories to come—and so it is with understanding and guessing. The hard will (the useful will) would only be a hindrance, and sometimes clearly is so. The inner activities of the will are specifically human capacities, which are as little inherited as speaking itself. The inner activities are guided by a receptive will; therefore one cannot and must not prescribe for one's will what is to be thought or remembered. (If one did so, it would already have been thought or remembered.) We give only the general direction. As with the capacities for inner activities of the will, expressive gestures are also nonbiological, that is, not inherited; they develop only in a normal human environment, and their form is culturally determined.[2]

From the characteristics described above, it is understandable why we call the expressive and receptive will the *gentle* will, and why we call the useful will, the goal-oriented will, or the work will, the *hard* will.

Like everything formed, the human body, too, consists of will. The will forces that move the body according to the will of the "I" become free from the physical body through the influence of the "I." The "I" is the source of communicative gestures that are specifically

---

consciousness attaches to their movement, in part. The stutterer "forgets" to do so when reciting someone else's text (as actors, for example) or when one sings the text to a melody. In *qi* exercises and others, we try to do the reverse of stuttering: to change the hard will into the gentle will.

2. It is well known that in many countries nodding and shaking the head mean just the opposite of their customary meaning in Europe.

human movements, such as eye contact, smiling, standing upright, walking, and speaking. The corresponding, partly unnamed *inner* activities of will develop in parallel with these movements.

When the expressive activity occurs from an inner impulse, not stimulated from without through an emotion or through egoism, then it comes closest to the true I. Then there arise deeds that are free, creative and intuitive (deeds of love). They are always simultaneously *witnessed*: thinking is understood; in singing, we hear in advance what is to be sung (as well as afterward); in pointing, we know to what it is that we point; in every art, there is a kind of imagining in advance, and (if vanity doesn't influence things) a kind of evaluation in retrospect.

The original connection of the "I" with the body takes place through expressive gestures. Everything else that we can observe in the small child in the way of reactions belongs in the arena of the sensitive body, a feeling automatism that guides biological processes in accordance with feeling, without conscious involvement. The vegetative nervous system is its bodily expression. If, for example, we sense danger, then the chemistry of the blood and the brain changes, along with pulse, blood pressure, and so forth.

The first will, in the development of the child as in the development of humanity, is the expressive-imitative will. The second is the expressive will. The third is the useful will.

The first will is operative in the small child, in early humanity, and in moments of inspiration. The second will in its double functioning can be applied variously. It can be active in a purely communicative (that is, creative) way out of the "I"; but it can also be misused in egoism. The third will is always bodily and serves usefulness or work. Since the Fall, work is always with us; the body is not solely the sign for changing meanings, not solely an expressive organ, but has needs of its own. Whatever we have to do of a noncommunicative character serves these needs. The work will can "tame" itself, can grow closer to the expressive will, by making its movements rhythmical; by accompanying them with music or singing; or by accompanying them with active fantasy. By imagining success, bodily achievements can be stimulated that would be impossible without this mental picture. Through these means, we try to give a meaning to the hard will, to make it similar to the gentle will.

In all three regions, in the regions of thinking, feeling, and willing, there are more or less fixed forms that are generally mixtures of the three soul functions. Thus, in addiction, a form of satisfaction is always accompanied by a mental picture at the outset; this wakens, in feeling, the memory of a pleasure, and this in turn triggers the will impulse to carry out the imagined act. Since addiction consists of the repetition of an act, the forms become ever more fixed, ever harder to dissolve.

Thoughts about the Will in Exercises of Attentiveness

Every exercise is an exercise of the will, including, therefore, exercises of concentration (thinking, mental picturing). The goal is to take the will into the exercise, so that the exercise is not being willed from without. The path of exercise begins with exercises of thinking/mental picturing, because this is the only autonomous inner activity. We normally begin such exercises for a reason that lies outside them, "so that...." There, the will is still outside the exercise. As long as it goes on this way, exercising remains an unpleasant duty, even if self-chosen. In creative activities, the will is *inside,* and so the activity becomes joy—the doing itself, not its result. This transformation can also happen in exercises of consciousness when concentration has reached a certain intensity—when thinking/mental picturing becomes so intense that attentiveness mostly flows into the activity itself. At the start, this is not the case at all.

The appearance of joy is at the same time the transition to improvisation in attentiveness. This means that memory retreats more and more, and allows space for the "Here and Now," in which every thought and every picture changes into thinking and "picturing," into a process—even if, *afterward*, we ascertain that the *content* of what was improvised isn't substantially different from previous exercises. *Purification* means steps toward the objectless state of a capacity, in which the capacity can exist more or less without objects. Objectlessness means receptive attentiveness, the reversed will, an attentiveness that is empty yet concentrated. As long as subconscious forms of thought, feeling, and will are still powerful, or exist at all, they will penetrate into awareness as associations when awareness attempts to become empty too soon (that is, without sufficient purity). In exercises of attentiveness, after a certain point there is nothing to strive after anymore. We simply allow *it* to come. This point is hard to describe or determine. Its characteristic feature is that attentiveness stays with the theme without "wanting" to, or that concentration begins to grow on its own. The precondition for this is the attainment of a certain degree of identification with the theme, a certain exclusiveness and depth of attention in the theme, similar to what can happen when attention immerses itself in an interesting, attractive theme. These are all simply parallel descriptions of the same state.

The more intuitive *and* pure that attention becomes, the more the will draws into thinking. Thinking, meanwhile, dissolves into cognitive feeling; now, the will draws into this feeling as well. If attention's intensity grows still further, feeling itself changes into willing—into the receptive will that is then imprintable from without. In meditation, the receptive will is imprintable by the next higher meaning of the thought, of the image, of the natural object.

At first, intensity and purity of attention seem to be in contrast to one another. It is normal for attentional intensity to arise with regard to a theme. This happens also in practices of attentiveness, up to the critical point of experiencing identity with the theme. From then on, the activity, the process of attentiveness, becomes ever more interesting, because it is being experienced directly. At the same time, the stream of attentiveness becomes ever more pure. The stream ends in the theme, but the experience happens before this endpoint; that is, we experience an ever purer attentiveness.

Contemplation / Meditation 26:
Identity nourishes the flow of attention.

EXERCISES OF THE WILL

Exercise 29

The second of the so-called supplementary exercises[3] deals with the will. It consists of carrying out a bodily activity at a previously determined point in time. The activity in question is "superfluous" (that is, you would not be doing it for any other reason); it is not useful. For example, you take off the ring from your finger and put

---

3. Steiner, *Founding a Science of the Spirit* (CW 95), lecture 12; see also Kühlewind, *From Normal to Healthy*, chapter 5.

it back on, or you walk diagonally through the room and then back. The best way is to decide each day the time of the next day's exercise, and perhaps also the activity one is going to perform. The activity can also remain the same, as long as it does not become automatic.

As the previous exercises, this one, too, is to be undertaken with concentrated attentiveness. This means that we follow its whole course consciously. It is helpful, here, that the activity has no practical purpose, so that the attentiveness is under no pressure to achieve, but can devote itself completely to the process itself. Concentration excludes automatic actions and every routinization, even when you repeat the same activity; you plan and survey the least detail as you carry it out. The more concentrated the attentiveness, the more every activity in consciousness is experienced as transparent; the true witness grows ever more present. We arrive at the experience that wakefulness, awareness, attentiveness *are* will. The more the slightest act of will is experienced, the more the sensation grows that the will that moves the hand or other parts of the body is not the will of the body; this will does not originate in the body, and is not, actually, *my* will. I simply guide it into the paths I have chosen. With this, it approaches in quality the expressive will; the doing itself becomes meaningful. This is independent from the content of what is done; whether I unbutton and then re-button a button, or move something on my desk from one spot to another, is not the essential thing. The meaning of the deed is difficult to describe, but we could put it this way. By consciously leading it, I take the will under my own command; I administer a will that actually does not belong to me. With this, we consciously integrate ourselves into the spiritual structure of the world, without losing individual independence or freedom.

Parenthetical Remark

The purification of the will begins when we have no other purpose in our act of will; we let it happen for its own sake. In *this sense,* every exercise is a will exercise. The more intensively our attentiveness is present in an exercise, the more "intelligent" the will becomes. It does not need to be led from without, through mental pictures or thinking (as in the hard will). Instead, the guidance that normally lies outside it draws within the will itself, dissolves into the will. What happens spontaneously in human creativity can, through this kind of practice, occur more easily and, therefore, more often. In this way, something cosmic appears in human creations, both as a general impulse of the time and culture, and as the individuality of the person doing the creating—giving form and direction to that impulse. In every act of creation there is a beginning; that is, creation is not caused by anything; it does not follow from anything; it is not a continuation of anything; it is completely autonomous. Human freedom, the autonomy of the will, culminates in meditation.

In creativity, we always notice a return to the original will that imitates immediately what it receives. This insight helps us to find the practices that can help us toward a creative life. The first will, which receives and reproduces, is given to us. It divides into two: the receptive and productive. In the gap between these two, the individual can operate, by guiding what has been received into creativity in an individualized way. This gap is the place of freedom. We can see this space of freedom in Michelangelo's painting in the Sistine Chapel, of the creation of Adam. God's and Adam's two index fingers point to one another, but do not touch.

Only the creative will is autonomous. Every other kind of will is stimulated from the outside—from outside the will itself. The will that is stimulated from outside is not my *own* will, in two different ways. We come to the experiential insight that we not only cannot create what is given to us in nature; we also can only administer (not create) thinking, feeling, and willing. "It thinks," "it feels," "it wills," become experiential through exercises of the will.

The exercises in Buddha's Eightfold Path are practices that dissolve habits. In them, we attempt *for the period of exercise* to carry out, with ever-increasing intensity, what we do everyday by habit, that is, with less than full awareness. Of course, these are also exercises of the will and, to a large extent, social exercises. Habits always contain the three components of thinking, feeling, and willing in a frozen conglomerate. Feeling carries the tone of "good-for-me"; thinking/mental picturing gives the habit a form; a trapped will delivers the compelling impulse to act.

All practices of the will are, initially, examples of the goal-bound will, since for the expressive will, as an intentional activity of willing, there is nothing to practice. *The goal of exercises of the will is the gradual transformation of the hard will into the gentle will.* This is also the case in exercises of concentration, since we try to do even these inner activities mostly with the hard will. Because, in every exercise, will plays a central role, every exercise can be seen as a path to the gentle will, which is the original will of the human being.

Exercise 30: Relaxation

The gentle will is relaxed. There are many techniques for relaxation, and almost all of them work with concentration on "parts of the body." The quotation marks here mean that we never notice the body itself, but only a sensation that surrounds the whole body, including what lies beneath the skin. Nevertheless, these exercises do work in a soothing way on the sensation of a bodily "covering," by releasing or diminishing cramps, knots, and blockages. The latter come about through mental, egotistical experiences of feeling, and can easily be transferred onto the body or its parts.

If one attempts to concentrate on the sensations in one part of the body, one soon realizes that this, too, cannot be accomplished through the hard will. This kind of will must be directed by thinking/mental picturing, and sensations cannot be thought or pictured—we must simply let them come. If we manage to have a sensation in a given body part, and if we can let it stay and/or become more intense through this "allowing" attentiveness, then we let it travel further through the different body parts, and finally try to feel the whole body at once. At this point, the reality of the observer or experiencer, the witness, begins to dawn on us slowly—the hidden goal of all attentional practices aimed at the body. The one who observes and experiences the sensations is not involved in them, and gradually separates out of the almost compulsive sense of identity with the body. However we arrive at this disengagement of the self, at its release from thinking, feeilng, and willing, we find that the true relaxation comes about through this Self alone. In parallel with this path of becoming a Self, the relaxed, gentle will appears with increasing intensity. As long as the "ego-I" is involved in mental tensions, techniques of relaxation work only for a short time. With relaxation exercises in art the situation is different; there, the element of the art in question helps the relaxation to last—at least for as long as the artistic activity itself lasts.

Exercises for the Gentle Will

Exercise 31: Speaking

The more consciously we speak (and consciousness here refers to the content of what is said), the more active our thinking seems to be. Logical, dialectical, rational thinking actually has an educational function, for the individual as well as for humanity. Its function is to correct the associative, subjectively colored flightiness of consciousness influenced by the subconscious, and to lead it back to intersubjective thinking—even if the latter is abstract, dead, and mechanical. This is conceptual thinking, which reasons from concept to concept in sequence. As we described before, thinking can develop further, into a more intuitive, concept-*forming* activity, and speech can then flow and be nourished from this source. This truly free speech may succeed initially for brief moments; the possibility for it depends, once again, on the concentratedness of consciousness, of attentiveness. When this concentratedness is directed toward the theme of speech, the disturbing components of the "ego-I," the murmurings of vanity, of the need to be right, grow ever fainter and fainter, until they disappear completely. When that happens, wordless, supralinguistic thinking flows forth without hindrance, and intuitively assumes the most appropriate form of speech. Here it is particularly clear that concentration has a moral quality.

Exercise 32: Remembering

A memory can be lifted into awareness only through the gentle will; you let the images, the thoughts, the feelings from "then" come up. There is no such thing as *one* memory; it is always a coherent tapestry of various qualities of the soul. They become livelier, more saturated with reality, the more we can "just let it happen." It is only the direction, the *what* of our intended memory, that is given by the "choiceful" will.[4] And we notice that the directive will and the memory itself are different from one another only when we have trouble bringing the memory up. Through the will that already "knows" what is to be remembered, we can determine with confidence whether the word, the name, and so forth, is the "right one" or not.

The exercise consists simply in trying to bring scenes, events, or images from the past into our awareness. At first, we choose more static images from the recent past, such as an image of a room or a landscape, and so forth. We allow the image to appear as exactly and as full of feelings as we can. By "feeling," we do not mean so much our own feeling reaction, but rather the feeling-tone that the image radiated (to the extent these two can be distinguished). This is why it is also useful first to bring up a global image, then perhaps to "look at" details within it.

It can be helpful, in exercises of memory, to have the conviction that *everything* we have experienced can be remembered. Actually, this includes what we have not experienced consciously—up to the point of the "great memory" of deep meditation (see below).

"Mechanical" exercises are often recommended to strengthen our memory (repetition of unconnected words or numbers, for example), but they use the hard will. They are not merely useless, but destructive, both for an organic memory that works from cognitive feeling and for the development of the gentle will.

---

4. On the "mechanism" of remembering, see Kühlewind, *The Life of the Soul*, chapter 4.

Once we are practiced in recalling static images from the recent past, we can try to awaken our memory of processes and events (again, from the recent past). There follow memories of the more distant past, first static, then process memories. It is advisable to start with images and events in which we are not involved. The more we reach into the far past, the more we run the risk of mixing memory and fantasy. If we pay attention in the first exercises (images from the recent past) to the sense of reality these memories have, then we will be able to distinguish between real memory and fantasy in distant memories as well. Fantasy elements are always more mobile, lightly shifting, in comparison with what is truly remembered.

These non-egoistic practices of memory give the practitioner the capacity to experience the process of remembering ever more deeply, since the content of memory is not the aim at all. It becomes experiential for us that the gentle will alone is active in memory, and we get a "feeling" for this kind of will, by which it becomes ever more attainable and applicable in various situations.

In principle, we can remember everything that we have experienced. Our attentional organism (the "I" in thinking, feeling and willing) carries out a certain inner gesture in every experience. To some degree, it becomes "that"—it becomes what we have experienced. In remembering, this organism repeats the same gesture. Since the gesture was not consciously desired during the experience, but happened through the receptive will, the hard will cannot "conform" to the experience in the same way. We can allow such a repetition to take place only through inner stillness—an undisturbed stillness, if possible.

Exercises of remembering use images and events that stem from our current earthly existence. In the chapter on the "Spiritual

Nature of Human Beings," we will talk about the possibility of another kind of "remembering"—the "great remembering."

Exercise 33: Imitation

The "imitative capacity" of the small child is based on the original receptive-reproductive will, the primal will. If an adult wants to imitate someone or something, he must reawaken this kind of will. Everyone who can imitate well (an actor, for instance) actually does so.

Conscious imitation of a movement is a small miracle, in the same sense as the imitation of sounds or words. For the sensory perception of the movement as a physical/physiological process bears no similarity to, and has no relationship to, the movements of the body that reproduce the movement. The simple fact that, in moving an arm, we perceive the form of movement through sight and the sense of movement (a difference from the case of hearing, in which we have no sensory perception of the motion of the speech organs) does not by itself help the muscles to reproduce what has been seen. It is evident that at the moment of seeing, our limbs lightly accompany the movements we see, just as the vocal chords and throat silently accompany what we hear.

Yet a good mimic works not merely from what he sees or hears of the person he is imitating. Sight and sound are only aids in finding the will that lies behind them. This is why the mimic by no means needs to have observed everything there is to observe in the person to be imitated. Once the will essence is grasped, then the mimic "knows" how the person smiles, gestures, walks, and so forth. It is all grasped through the primal will that is, normally, scarcely available to adults. Imitative practices begin with external imitation. You observe a person's movements, or some motion in nature, and attempt to reproduce it. For this kind of observation, the right glance to use is *global*—that is, if possible, we use the receptive will and not the analytic glance, which is our normal starting point. With repeated imitation, a kind of feeling that guides the imitative movements comes ever more to the fore. Finally, through the growing sense of identification with what we observe, the receptive will appears. Since we cannot imitate by using the hard will, such practices are appropriate for strengthening the gentle will.

Exercise 34: Reading

In reading something written in letters, static spatial forms (in this case, two-dimensional forms) are transformed into hearable forms.[5] This is the precondition for reading. In reality, we "read together" the vocal sounds moving in time into words; we read the words together into sentences; we read the sentences together into still larger, meaningful wholes. And it is these largest units from which the sentences, words, and sounds (in just this descending order) have their origin. We also read together these elements when we hear someone speak.

With simple, informative texts, we have no problem of understanding. However, we certainly do have such problems with more demanding texts, which offer us new thoughts and stimulate new thoughts within us. We have to do justice to this kind of stimulation, or we have the feeling of having missed something. We can only read such texts slowly, and with the gentle will (in this case, the receptive will). As an example of this kind of reading we can use a text from the posthumous work of Thrasybulos Georgiades:

---

5. Kühlewind, "The Perception of Spatial and Temporal Forms," *Goetheanum*, May 20, 1984.

> We will call that which makes up a human being *nous*. My theme
> is how this *nous* is active when it *notices*. What does it notice? A
> duality: on the one hand *things*, on the other hand *what lasts*. The
> *lasting* permeates consciousness. Things remain outside; they
> are and remain an Outside. *The lasting* penetrates so very much
> into *nous* that *nous* cannot be thought of apart from it. *The lasting*
> constitutes *nous*. Yet *nous* is not identical with *the lasting*, which
> is rather its anchor, the ground on which it rests, the element in
> which it lives and weaves, and by which it is permeated.[6]

The exercise consists in the reader's contemplating these sentences one after the other, and then all (or some) in their inter-
relatedness. "What makes up the human being," the *nous*, is the
specifically human attentiveness or wakefulness (awareness),
which can direct itself to anything, even to things. Things are
everything that appears to *nous* as finished, as a fixed form—
objects, then, whether sense perceptible things or thoughts,
feelings, fantasies. *The lasting* is not experienced as an object,
just as *nous* itself is not. Actually, all difficulties of understanding in regard to processes come from the *nous* being able to perceive with clarity only things. Movements, processes, however,
require the experience of *the lasting*, if these are really understood. Yet in changes, movements, *the lasting* is experienced
only dimly. Nor do we experience attentiveness or wakefulness,
but only their objects—like things.

The process of pondering over these sentences could be extended.
We ponder or contemplate using the gentle will. In the same way,
during the period of exercise we can slow down our *learning* itself,
and make it more inward (for example, when we study subjects in
mathematics or natural science). This kind of reading and learning

6. *Nennen und Erklingen: Die Zeit als Logos* (Naming and Speaking: The Time
as Logos), Göttingen: Vandenhoeck & Ruprecht, 1985.

are parts of a general project: the slowing down of life.[7] Speaking, imitating, learning, and reading are all activities of consciousness in which the gentle will is responsible, and in which the hard will is an obstacle. The following exercises address activities that are initially the province of the hard will, and attempt to move them in the direction of the expressive will.

Exercise 35: The Body

Normally, work done by the body is carried out by the hard will. If the work is rhythmic, or if it can be made so, then the introduction and maintenance of a rhythm is known to be helpful for the workers. All the songs that accompany various forms of work point in this direction; and so does the activity of fantasy that accompanies any work. Through this "accompaniment," the work approaches an activity of the gentle will, as if the situation were reversed. The song, the rhythm, the events in the fantasy become the central event, and the bodily work becomes the accompanying activity. It is as if we accompany the rhythm of the song with work. Our attentiveness has to stay with the work in part (for example, while peeling potatoes). But attention is also partly with the singing or with the imagined events. Every kind of bodily work can be transformed in this way, and then it becomes easier, less tiring, and more effective.

Mental picturing also plays a big role in sports, and is especially effective in high jumps and in long distance running. In Zen archery, the use of the gentle will and an imaginative awareness is well known. Here we approach an area of practice that was originally conceived as a kind of therapy, and later was applied in

---

7. Kühlewind, *Die Diener des Logos*, Stuttgart, 1981, chapter 5.

the Zen martial arts. A few exercises from *qi* practice can serve as examples. In these, we can see that the gentle will is stronger than the hard will even in a bodily sense, and that mental pictures play a central role in it.

Exercise 36: Qi (Chi)

A. These exercises are done in pairs. Your partner holds your arm with two hands. Try to free your arm with muscular force. If your partner is strong enough (and he should be), you will find that you cannot free it. After several unsuccessful attempts, direct your whole attention to your other hand, or to something that you see (a picture, a landscape); or else hum a tune (with full attention), and without using muscular force, free your arm. When you draw your attention "out" from the arm being held, your partner can notice that you are "no longer there." All these exercises are successful when you are somewhat concentrated—that is, when you can manage your own attentiveness. To free the arm, you do not apply your normal will, which is tied strongly to self-feeling.

B. Your partner holds a stick with both hands at one end, the other end pointing horizontally in front of him or her. Touch the tip of your index finger to the other end of the stick and try to push your partner backward through the stick. This can hardly be successful. Now stand on one foot, lifting the other. In this position, it is completely hopeless to push your partner backward through the stick by muscle power alone. Your partner is standing on two feet, so when you push it is you who falls backward. Now, however, imagine that you are pointing at something behind your partner with the index finger touching the stick, or that your partner is being pulled backward by the collar. You do not *want* to shove the other back at all; you are only making a pointing gesture with your arm and reaching out. Your partner falls backward.

You can also proceed by shifting your attention to the other hand. Surprisingly, the pointing hand becomes incomparably stronger.

C. Your partner stands in front of you, and you try to shove her or him sideways with your arm and hand, first with muscle power. Your partner resists; it is a physically difficult task on your side. Now imagine a light sideways movement with your arm and hand—for example that you are sweeping dry leaves from a table. Your partner will fall over or shift sideways.

In these exercises, it is important always to try with the hard will first. With this, we collect our whole egoism, our me-feeling, in this one point. This changes when our attention goes to the other hand (or wherever), and the hand that we are doing something with regains the original will power that is free of egoism.

These and many other *qi* exercises serve, above all, to make us familiar with the "taste" of the gentle will. After some exercise (perhaps after much exercise), we can evoke and apply this gentle form of movement even without mental pictures. From these experiences, we can begin to guess that the original human will is the expressive will. The hard will is weaker, because in it the me-feeling (as the basis of egoism) overshadows and stifles the original will.

Parenthetical Remarks

If we pursue the concentration exercise (7) beyond the second I AM experience (that is, if the intensity of attentiveness grows still further), then the Self or Self-Consciousness continues, but changes gradually into a will-consciousness. "I am will" would be the meditative expression of this.

A sketch of the process would look like this:

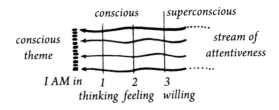

Beyond 3., the process has no limits.

The anthropological genealogy of forms of will can be summarized as follows:

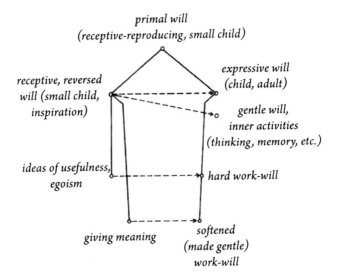

FOURTH PRELUDE

We do not know.... We scarcely notice what we have been given and how richly.

For whenever we do not notice *how* we do something, we are being given a gift.

Thinking, feeling, willing (in the cognitive and creative sense), understanding, being oriented toward the good (otherwise, we would not even know what is "good for me"), having senses, living in the light, being able to reflect, having access to a universal attentiveness.... did we do anything to get all this, did we work for it?

It is all a gift—and, through it, the whole objective world. From where? From whom? Why? And for what? So richly gifted.

Why then is there so much suffering and bitterness in the human world?

What is to be done?

IV.

The Spiritual Nature of Human Beings

The Cosmic Background of the Gentle Will

What "makes up the human being," to quote Thrasybulos Georgiades, is our attention, our spiritual being. By "spiritual" we mean two things. What is spiritual is matter-free and meaningful. Meanings are matter-free[1] and, therefore, so are understanding and the one who understands.

Contemplation / Meditation 27:
A triangle becomes a tetrahedron when the true subject can
experience the three angles simultaneously, as if from above.

understanding

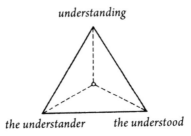

the understander   *the understood*

Whatever is matter-free is also free of space and time. The spiritual essence of the human being, spaceless and timeless, extends over the entire world of meanings (the *rupa* world, or lower *devachan*) and over the world of "I" beings (*arupa* world, or upper *devachan*)

---

1. See Kühlewind, *Meditationen: Über Zen-Buddhismus, Thomas von Aquin und Anthroposophie*, chapter 1.

who make and understand meanings.[2] If, as human beings, our spiritual essence were the whole of our being, we would simply be continuations of various spiritual entities and completely dependent on them. This dependence is avoided because a portion of our spirituality dwells in the material body. Originally, the spirit used that body as its tool for expression in the material, sensorially perceptible world. The function of the physical body, however, is intended to separate the spirit in the human being from the spiritual world, to the extent that we are bound to the body, which becomes a secure anchor for us, allowing us to resist being moved about by the winds of spirit.

What we now call "the capacity to imitate" is a vestige of the primal characteristic of the cosmic human being, who was still a part of the spiritual cosmos. We can still find its image in archaic cultures, in which everything, even activities of the body (eating, drinking, procreation, birth, death) were sacred events—that is, signs for meanings. Meaning regulated life, not usefulness and comfort.[3] All work was sacred, that is, oriented toward meaning, and so physical movements were expressive, and carried out by the gentle will.

The profaning of life began with the appearance of religions (as signs), into which meaning retreated and lived on, now separate from everyday life. Earlier, everyday life was itself sacred, so there was no sense in speaking of religion or spirituality. With time, everyday life fell more and more under the spell of usefulness, because it slid into an egoism that took hold of religion as well. Spiritual power confused itself with worldly power. In our

2. Sanskrit: *rupa* = form; *arupa* = form-free.
3. Kühlewind, *Das Licht des Wortes,* chapter 5.

time, religion has come to the very edge of everyday life, and even attempts at restoring religion (fundamentalisms) are drenched permeated by the principle of usefulness.

Imitation, or "becoming-*that*," if it were to happen utterly, would mean the end of cognition. There would be no witness present who, in order to remain a witness, did *not* go along, did *not* become what is being "imitated." The separation from the spiritual world or world of meanings shrinks this kind of adaptation, or "becoming-*that*," to a homeopathic level (apart from the sphere of speaking and singing). Through the anchor of the physical body, this separation makes possible the steadiness of the witness and (therefore) of cognition.

In prehistoric times, the human being was originally all meaning (or all sensory organ),[4] just as we can assert today of the small child. This *single* sense was capable of grasping another I-being immediately, and is still the "highest" sense for today's adult. Now, however, the activity of this "You-sense" is no longer immediate, but mediated through other senses such as our sense for thinking, for the word, for vowels, for movement (perceptually), for sight, and for sound, as well as through the inward versions of the other senses (the senses of balance, touch, warmth, taste, and smell). The way in which the various senses operate *today* is the result of many successive alterations.[5]

The active versions of these senses are particularly new; the sense of speech, for example, perceived the signs of nature or of divinity in primal eras passively (just as the infant first appropriates language), learning to understand with the *whole* of attentiveness while still unable to speak. The bodily organs for the

---

4. Steiner, *The Riddle of Humanity* (CW 170), lectures 7 and 14.
5. Ibid., lecture 7.

"you-sense," the thinking sense, and the speech sense are not as localizable as the eye or ear; they extend over the entire resting body (in the case of the "You-sense"); over the life-organism at rest (thinking-sense); and over the movement-organism at rest (speech-sense). A portion of each of these organisms effects the corresponding activity: the throat, as the part of the movement-organism, for speaking; a portion of the life-organism for thinking. Our "*I-ing*" is still not perfect: all the parts of the body that serve enjoyment maintain this imperfection.[6]

Through the me-feeling, all these changes serve human independence, and so, in the final analysis, serve the possibility of self-development to the true I-being, the true Self. What we call the path of knowledge, the schooling of consciousness, the inner path, and so forth, is an attempt to integrate the spiritual aspect of the human being, which has remained cosmic, through the intensification of I-consciousness. It is an attempt to lift consciousness into the region that is still, for now, supraconscious. The intensification of I-consciousness means that it requires less and less reliance on what is given (such as our bodies) in order to *be*.

Exercise 37: Being Silent

Adults can notice that their consciousness is never silent—at least, not while awake. In the exercise of "right speech" from the eightfold path, external silence is made easier by the practice of observing the speech of one's partner.[7] Right speech is already a very demanding exercise, which can be deepened infinitely. Yet being silent is even harder, since the practitioner has no partner to listen to. External silence is only the very beginning, which can

---

6. Ibid., lecture 14.
7. Kühlewind, *From Normal to Healthy,* chapter 4.

and should be extended to inner silence. Two of its traits should be mentioned. Why, after all, is it so hard to establish the inner "sea-calm" (Buddha's expression)? It is because, through our inner dialogue, we keep our accustomed world going; and we solidify it all the more through every thought we think in the words of a given language. We are accustomed to think in words, and this habit nails us down to a certain level of consciousness (to the past, in fact), unless we can think consciously and meditatively. Poetic texts make up an intermediate level between information and meditation. The habitual human clings with every ounce of strength to the world of the past, to the everyday world, and by no means wants to leave this world, this consciousness.

It is obvious that peace in consciousness cannot be attained by an act of this same consciousness.[8] Such an act would only change the content of consciousness. For the motion, the inner noise, to become quieter, the level of consciousness has to rise. Word thinking has to be left behind, for the more fluid, wordless, concept-free "thinking" to enter. Consciousness has to rise through a continuum of growing stillness, until it reaches complete silence. This continuum is often described as a series of stages.

As long as consciousness has not yet reached complete silence (emptiness), the constant whisperings of spirit in the supraconscious spirit of the human being cannot be heard. Inner stillness can also grow beyond the stage of complete silence and reach the point of "negative" stillness, which is even quieter than the

---

8. The expressions "to extinguish a content" and "to empty consciousnesss" are instructions that cannot be fulfilled by ordinary consciousness. Rather, during practice they occur through the gentle will—you could say, spontaneously. In making music, too, the instructions (for example, "crescendo," or "ritardando") should not be thought, but simply carried out. If we think them, we fall out of the stream of the music.

absence of sound: a receptive, vessel-like stillness. The deeper it is, the higher the inspiration that can be perceived. The stillness (at whatever level) need not last long in time. For the timelessness that shines into this stillness can reveal infinitely much in the fraction of a second. A person can then work for years on what was revealed in that fraction of a second. If the stillness is present, you can be sure the Holy Spirit is within it. This conviction is the background of the silent religious services of the Quakers. It is also the test of any human group: if they can be silent together for ten minutes, then they are a community.

This great, negative silence, this waiting without aim or purpose, and the inspiration that appears within it, demonstrate the nature of the receptive-reproductive expressive will. It reinstates the original connection with spirituality; the otherwise supraconscious roots of the human being are lit up by the "I." We ensure the formation or awakening of the true Self by having the path of schooling proceed, always, by means of the purified will of the individual.[9] At the same time, the cultivation of silence is a path of purification from all pre-formed contents.

Experience shows that memory happens best through "letting come" what we have gone through in our lives. At this point it can also occur to us that we can "remember" something that doesn't belong to the experiences and events of our human lives, but is the content/event of the timeless, spiritual world. This is the "Great Remembering." Plato maintained that every cognition is such a memory, of the given world. However, spiritual research goes beyond this in every sense, and can remember truths that do not belong at all to our current picture of the world.

---

9. Kühlewind, *Aufmerksamkeit und Hingabe*, chapter 19.

Meditation

What can happen passively in silence (that the heavens open because the soul opens) is pursued in an active sense in meditation. Meditation consists in concentrating oneself on themes that have a special quality; their informational meaning is like a veil behind which lies hidden a deeper or higher meaning. If one aims at this higher meaning (that is, if one concentrates on it), then it reveals itself once more as the next veil of a still higher meaning, and so on, forever. To grasp a higher meaning is not thinking or understanding in the normal sense, but an experience. In everyday life, words and concepts conceal experience; instead of experiencing something, the corresponding word or concept is ready and we do not bother to actually have the experience. In meditating, there are *only* experiences, or it was not a meditation at all. Experiences change us; thoughts and understandings of the normal kind do not, or only to a very modest degree. For the person who has been changed in this way, through meditation, the "same" theme says something different the second time from what it said the first time. What was experienced in meditation as the higher meaning on one occasion assumes the form of a veil for a second attempt. In meditating, we move from form, through a momentary emptiness, to a higher form. All forms are preliminary to a higher meaning.[10]

Exercise 38: Sentence Meditation

The light is the I AM: form-free.

The first step, to prepare the meditation, is contemplation or pondering. This means thinking about the words of the sentence, and perhaps even its grammatical connections, in a concentrated,

---

10. Kühlewind, *From Normal to Healthy*, chapter 5.

deepened way. What kind of light? How can it be identical with the I AM? What does "form-free" mean and what is the function of freedom from form? And so on. What does the word "is" mean in this sentence?

Contemplation (or pondering) has three functions. First, it exhausts thinking in the sense of tiring it out and in the sense of causing it to experience its own impotence with regard to the sentence. Through contemplation, we try to prevent thinking from being active during meditation itself, when it should be silent. Second, contemplation on the words and the grammatical construction of the sentence mostly takes place through wordless thinking, which is then used in meditation. Third, in contemplation a new insight may arise that becomes the best point of entry into meditating, not only because of its content, but also through the opening by which the insight arrived.

Contemplation spontaneously leads over into *reduction*, in which the sentence appears as a unity. Either one can draw together all the words into a single word that then represents the sentence as a whole, or one can "glue" the words together as if the sentence consisted in a single word. Through meditative practice, there grows a capacity to experience the sentence as a unity right away, without previous inner activity. Meditation is the concentration of attention on this unity. If the sentence remains a sequence of words, one cannot concentrate on the meaning of the sentence.

It is essential for meditation that we "forget" all associations, all thinking, all goals, and also all feelings at the level of sympathy and antipathy. Attention becomes the theme, exclusively. With sufficient concentration, the sentence (the meaning of the sentence, which is the theme) loses its given form for an instant, as if it melted or became transparent. A new "form," insight, understanding, emerges as our experience. The light (in the sentence just given) becomes a higher form, on the level of pure, super-linguistic "thinking." If during practice, you can linger in this kind of "thinking," your experience changes and enters a new level.

This "thinking" is much closer to a certain kind of pictoriality than is everyday thinking. It can also happen that an image appears as the new meaning, as an "insight." Yet this pictoriality is in no way similar to mental pictures or fantasy images. The light, the I AM, cannot be represented in a normal way at all; it is a question of living, nonstatic images that derive from a kind of feeling. Every image, even a geometrical figure, is based on feeling as if its static form becomes alive. This dawning pictoriality shifts into an experience of feeling.

Feeling is already contained like a seed within the words *light, is, I am, and "form-free."* This feeling has nothing to do with the vocal structure of the words, but is incorporated in the meaning of the words.

At this stage, when the sentence begins to be "feelable," the practitioner can initiate a second kind of contemplation in feeling. You "ponder" or "contemplate" the individual words in feeling, then try to experience the whole sentence as a living feeling-form. If this succeeds, you concentrate in feeling on this living and weaving feeling-form. As mentioned above, we have no words for these qualities within feeling; they are cognitive, and unapproachable for our thinking. In feeling-concentration on a whole sentence, the feeling-form can melt again and a further feeling can light up.

Once you have experienced the whole sentence as a feeling-form, *then* the feeling-forms of the individual words light up as well. "Light" becomes a feeling, "form" becomes a feeling, and even "free" becomes a feeling in the *interconnectedness* of the sentence as a whole. You recognize the *meaning* of the words, in their origin, as feelable.[11]

The second stage of meditation takes place in cognitive feeling. The result is an inspiration. In reality, there are no stages, but only a continuous progression.[12]

When, as a meditant, you experience the sentence as a feeling-form, you will experience yourself as a unique utterance in feeling—as being a Self at the level of cognitive feeling. But the whole world as well, and the light that "illumines" the world and makes it capable of being experienced, become feeling. "Everything is feeling"—that is the experience. This feeling, that is the world, can be experienced in feeling only by someone who feels. The suspension of separateness, already experienced at the level of life (living, pure thinking) is heightened here still further. Even in everyday life, we are not separate in our feelings; an experience of feeling is not an object. Moreover, those who experience it are is not subjects; they *are* the feeling.

At every "level," you can repeat the same theme endlessly with new insights and understandings of the same quality each time. This can take place, for example, at the level of pure thinking or at the level of cognitive feeling. The heightening of the level of consciousness, like every other "method" used within meditation, goes best when it happens "spontaneously" and, of course, never

---

11. The words in a meditation sentence are used in their primal meaning. Such primal meaning makes possible all the applications of a given word. For example, the word *in* can be used in spatial, temporal, and metaphorical senses ("in friendship," for example). What makes all the applications possible is the primal meaning, the kind of meaning grasped by a small child.

12. Kühlewind, *Die Wahrheit Tun*, chapters on "The Purity of Striving," and "The Second Level of Meditation."

according to the intention of everyday consciousness. The latter ought not to interfere in with the inner event, which is a cosmic process, a process of the world of meanings, a part of which is the supraconscious nature of the human being. The gradual "awakening" of this supraconscious nature means to gradually become self-aware and therefore cognizing within the spiritual world—the world of meanings and I-beings.

In meditative undertakings, the will is always the gentle will. You "let it happen"; but this *letting* is the very greatest human activity. The gentle will is cultivated and applied for the sake of an ever greater silence, so that the Quiet may be heard; for the sake of an ever more peaceful "non-doing," so that it may occur. The more "my will" can retreat, the more strongly we can experience the will that burns toward us from the outside, from the sense world, from the soul world, from the spirit world, in everything that has form.

Slowly, the feeling-form of our sentence turns into a will-form. *Light* becomes will. The *I AM, form, form-free*, become forms of will, and so does the one who perceives them or, better, the one who *experiences them*. Will can be experienced only through *receptive* will, and if we experience it we *become* receptive will—form-free, so that we can adapt to all forms and yet remain a form-free self. This is the paradoxical fundamental characteristic of I-beings. They can become everything, and remain completely unchanged. At the same time, you can feel that you have approached the source of the will, and become identical with it bit by bit. In full understanding, you experience the I-being whose will it is.

Once the will-quality of a meditation theme begins to dawn, then the practitioner tries to "ponder" the words of the sentence in regard to their will-form, then to concentrate on the whole sentence as will, in the deep silence of the receptive will—the empty will, if possible. Purification, like attentiveness, can be heightened without limit. The process of finding meaning, the dissolution of what has been found as a veil before the next moment of finding, can go forward endlessly. This is what it means to enrich creation through the creation of new meanings. Every creative human and non-human individual creates from out of the same source: from the Logos. And every creation is individual, individualizing its creator, since what we draw from this source is not something finished and formed. In the end, the human creator gives it a form, and therefore creations have individual style.

The path has no end. Complete purification (from sensory forms, whose origin is me-feeling, egoism) shifts over into creative giving, into the second, creative love.[13] Here, the Logos shows its essence, already seen by Heraclitus, in increasing by itself: whoever gives, receives. Whoever gives more, receives more. Giving love makes love richer.

Exercise 39: Image Meditation

In describing meditation on a sentence, it is clear that the original unity of a text is the sentence. From the meaning of the sentence, the words and grammar are "chosen" (the choosing rarely takes place consciously). The source is always unity, oneness. Concepts arise through the selective attention, which turns from the unity toward its parts. The fact that there are parts is already the result of the selective attention, which always works with the help of *looking aside*, of *not taking into account*, in order to form concepts that are always both more narrow and more distinct.

---

13. Kühlewind, *Die Esoterik des Erkennens und Handelns*, chapter 6.

In meditation with symbolic images, we go through this process in reverse. Just as meditative sentences generally do not express given truths, but truths that must be realized in the course of meditating,[14] symbolic images do not represent given perceptual realities. Instead, they are the irreducible expression of spiritual realities that generally have to be made real in meditating them. They are irreducible to *other* forms of expression, such as thoughts or texts.

As an example, we can try this image: A desert, hot and dry, and in it a rose stem with a red rose in bloom.

The first time we do this meditation, we cannot remember such an image, but can only build it up or let it build itself up from its elements. First, a desert landscape, then in one spot the rose stem rising, with leaves and a bud that turns into a red blossom. If we use this image as theme for meditation more frequently, then it is best not to call up earlier mental pictures of the image from memory, but to build it up afresh each time, as if for the first time, and even with new details. Here we can't proceed from the whole; we arrive at the whole by building it up. Once it's there, then we can ponder its elements: the desert, the sand, the rockiness of it, then the growth of the plant, and so forth. In all this, the unreality of the composition gains a meaning. After pondering (that is, after exhausting our conceptualities), we try simply to hold the image with an inner, questioning gesture (if possible, without thinking). Like the meditative sentence, the image, too, can reveal itself as the veil in front of a meaning.

---

14. For example, "In thinking, I experience myself at one with the stream of cosmic occurrence." Steiner, *The Threshold of the Spiritual World* (CW 17), chapter 1.

Since every image consists in a feeling, which lies hidden behind concepts, we try to reach the feeling of the image. In concentration, if it is deep enough, we can learn to leave behind words and concepts. Then all that remains is the pure *that*—the experience of the movement that could lead to the concept. What remains is thus an identity with the pure *that*. There is no concept for the image; otherwise it would not be a meditative image but an emblem or concept.

The experience that leads to the next meaning, in the case of meditative images, takes place within feeling. In feeling, meanings can arise that cannot be translated into words or thoughts. Meditating, the act of meditation itself, becomes the rose blooming in the desert of non-feeling; this is a partial, approximate formulation, and even a thousand others could not exhaust the image or adequately reproduce it.

The image and its elements have evidently come about through a kind of will, and are also "held" through the same will. The more intensively we feel the image, the more this feeling metamorphoses into a sense for the will that lives within the image. As with every will, we attempt to approach its source. In the end, every meditation leads to a being, and through it to the highest I-being, from which we breathe in the spirit; it leads to the Logos that has become human.

Exercise 40: Perceptual Meditation

In perceptual meditation, [15] we always take for our theme a natural object or phenomenon whose idea, whose meaning, is unattainable for thinking (in contrast to exercises of concentration with

---

15. Kühlewind, *Die Belehrung der Sinne.*

a fabricated object). In this kind of meditation, we try to awaken cognitive feeling within our perception. This kind of feeling is present in the first moment of eye contact, and in how we look at a human face. It is a global look; we recognize a face without being able to say anything about its details.

We try to look at a piece of gravel, a leaf, a tree, a flower, and so forth, with this global, receptive look, and to avoid all concepts as far as possible. This means that we have to have already largely mastered our thinking, our associating, and everything that tends to "occur" to us. We try to pay attention only to the feeling and the will that radiate out from the theme. We let ourselves be imprinted by this radiance that lives in the things of nature. All this happens, initially, while looking at the object. Through practice, we can intensify cognitive feeling to the point of being able to feel the object's quality without any sense perception. This is how archaic people feel. They often do not know how a natural object looks, because they do not perceive it with the physical senses. Many spiritual healers, too, "feel" diagnostically with their eyes closed—seeing would only interfere with their feeling. *What* we feel is really a kind of will. In perceptual meditation, as in the other kinds of meditation, thinking, feeling, and willing operate in a continuum; the reality of nature lies above the level of pure thinking. Contact between the perceiver and the theme begins in feeling.

If the I AM experience has been achieved through exercises of attentiveness, then it can also be attained in perceptual exercises. Here, attention becomes lastingly receptive, and lets itself be imprinted by the perceptual theme. It grows stronger and perceives itself in this very process of being imprinted—*as* a process, as a feeling process, as a process of reversed will. In some cases, the Self may also arise for the first time in intensive perceptual practices.

Exercise 41: Meditation with a Question or Meditative Research

All the reports of spiritual researchers have their source in meditative research. This means *spiritual* research, which can occur through meditation in thinking, in images, or in perception. It depends on the point of departure that the researcher chooses for a question or problem. The form (thought, text, or image) offers the theme of one's concentration.

Let us take psychological problems as an example. The first senseless, meaningless form in the human being (that is, the first noncommunicative form), is the me-feeling, the kernel of egoism.[16] The me-feeling is, initially, like a coat that covers the whole body. Generally, it is mistaken for a feeling of the body. However, as modern human beings, we feel our bodies no more than we feel a piece of wood or a stone. Cognitive feeling would feel the *meaning* of the body or of its parts, but this is hindered by the cloak of me-feeling. Feeling and sensation can perceive only feeling and sensation, not things, bodies, objects.

The me-sensation is an experience, and therefore it is the object of an attentiveness that is still without any subject. Through it, other meaningless forms come about in the soul. Partly, such addictions are connected to various biological functions of the body that become sources of pleasure: fine eating, smoking, and so forth. The biblical Fall is described as the first case of eating for the sake of pleasure (without meaning), and eating then becomes the prototype and symbol of gestures and behaviors that have no

---

16. Kühlewind, *Aufmerksamkeit und Hingabe,* chapters 7, 13, 18.

expressive function, that are not communicative, that say nothing, that do not *mean*.[17] We can understand these forms without much trouble, since they are bound to the body. But there are other meaningless mental forms that have nothing to do with the body, such as envy, vanity, lust for power, hate, anger, and so forth, and whose satisfaction is certainly pleasurable, but not localizable on the body. At most, their effects relate to the body indirectly. How do these forms come about? That is to be our research problem.

We take an image as our meditative theme, because processes in sensation are inaccessible for thinking and (especially) for language. The latter are too coarse to describe the nature of this sphere of the soul. Our image, then, is a husk that surrounds the human body. It has an indefinite thickness with an indistinct edge, and its surface is like a cloud without contours. We take this image from the experience of exercises 19 and 20, with their attempt to sense a finger or the whole body. We also know that this self-enclosed husk arose from a formation of spokes or *radii*. The rays that originally were directed outward from a center, and back again toward this center (reproductive and receptive), have transformed themselves partially into this closed form.

We build up this mental picture, and try to "contemplate," in feeling, the change from an arrangement in *radii* to the form of the husk. We also ponder the consequences for the relationship of human beings to their environment. Then we concentrate on this image.

We can perceive that the tendency that produced the closed form continues within it. This perception is determined by how we feel the form, and by its effect on the human being. First,

---

17. In its celebration of Mass, Christianity attempts to "redeem" eating, to reinstate its meaning through the ingestion of bread and wine.

further contours or inclusions come about that correspond to (we could say that *surround*) the various parts of the body. But then there develop smaller pieces, independently, from out of the unitary husk, as if a great ball transformed itself into many littler ones. You feel that the movement that caused the husk form to derive from the radiating form is working on in these smaller pieces. You also feel that this process will roll on endlessly, if nothing is done to stop it.

Meaningless mental formations can be arranged typologically; despite bearing the same name, however, no two are actually identical, not even within a single person. Vanity, for example, can relate to the beauty of the face, to a sports achievement, or to scientific success. These vanities vary greatly in their nature, in how they feel; only the term for them is the same. And so it is with other formations; they are partly biographical, partly inborn tendencies. Without egoism, they don't come to the fore; they all apply to that substitute for the true Self. They form, and are, this substitute. Ultimately, they are all noncommunicative forms within the soul, whether or not they use the body for their satisfaction.

All these "senseless" forms relate to the "substitute-I" or substitute Self. Its kernel is the me-feeling, and habits of the soul (in thinking, feeling, and willing) grow from this kernel. So does the external biography that we remember and to which we relate our experiences. The true Self would be, or is, a witness who actually sees, *experiences*, the soul's fluctuations. This means participation and knowledge of the experience, and therefore independence from it.

If, in meditation, an imagistic understanding has been reached, then one can begin to attend to feeling—that is, to notice the feeling that has always been present. The transition here, like every transition in our practice, happens spontaneously. The radiating, straight lines of light that both illumine and perceive what has been illumined have one feeling-tone. The bent-back "rays" that sense nothing else, but sense only themselves (and this kind of sensation comes into the world through these rays; they *are* this sensation)—these bent-back rays have a different quality, a darkening within feeling. Compared to the light, every form is darkness. This experience in feeling can be condensed more or less in the (meditative) sentence: Nothing more is illuminated. Or: Nothing more is given. It is not a pleasant experience in feeling. The whole negative, diseased, humanly unworthy character of egoism imposes itself on the experiential feeling. For the person who goes through this, egoism has already lost the positive function it had in earlier phases of life. This meditation has a similarity to what is described as the encounter with the "guardian of the threshold."[18]

The dark and threatening character of egoism, which we never notice in normal consciousness, becomes in this meditation an almost unendurable, shocking experience at the level of feeling. A portion of the shock is caused by the insight that such a thing can remain hidden from everyday consciousness. The threat soon makes itself felt as a quality of will, and this leads to a further change in the meditation. The theme, the original image, changes into a will-form. It changes into something, or rather into some-*one*. Through the reversed will, we perceive a will that *wants* this self-involvement of the originally radiant light. Now the elements of the image are "investigated" as to their will-character, through

---

18. Steiner, *How to Know Higher Worlds* (CW 10), the capter entitled "The Guardian of the Threshold."

the reversed will that allows itself to be imprinted by them. If, then, the image is meditated as a will-form, there appears in this will a *who*. The being that "inspires" egoism, or the senseless forms that generally seem to have a useful purpose, is thus experienced—at least at the periphery and to the extent of seeing that there is someone there. This wellbeing is neither uniformly negative nor positive (all such expressions are far from adequate to the complexity of the experience). The self must become completely independent of forms (in the moments of meditation) to be able to deal appropriately with this figure—with its will.

It is clear that meditation on a question (meditative research) consists in the practitioner's or researcher's bringing the question into a meditatable form (a sentence, an image) to give the procedure a direction. Then, in growing silence, we wait and we watch.

For further meditations, see appendix.

SENTENCE AND IMAGE MEDITATIONS

SENTENCES

The world is light.
The light illuminates itself.
Nothing is in the light.
Everything disappears tracelessly into the light.
This is light.
What should the light illumine?
I am the light.
Only the I AM can experience the light.
The I is form-free.
The Self is only now.
I am in between.
Everything is now.
The I AM divinity is active now.
In seeing, subject and object are suspended.
The seer becomes reality.
We hover between body and spirit, without experiencing them.
Attention is identity.
From identity comes imitation.
Me or I.
We remember objects.
Images come from out of seeing.
Words replace experience.

Images

The New Testament is full of images that can all be meditated. For example: The sower, as told in Mark 4, with all the details of that chapter; the scene at the pool of Bethesda, as told in John 5.2–9.

Buddha's Flower Sermon: instead of speaking words, the Buddha holds up a flower.

In a landscape, there stands a wall with a closed door.

Isaiah 40:3–4, compared with Matthew 3:3.

Reversal of the Will
and Encountering the Power
of the Logos

In chapter 5 ("Outlook") of Rudolf Steiner's *Riddle of the Human Being*,[1] he writes about the fundamental experience of passing "from thinking to the *experience* of thinking." In normal consciousness, it is not thinking that is experienced, but (through thinking) that which is thought. The same process is insisted upon in the second half of *The Philosophy of Freedom*.[2] By devoting oneself again and again to thoughts through a certain *will*, one can perceive forces of the soul "that can be discovered only in *conscious* application." A spiritual awakening is brought about through the experience of thinking itself. The use of the will, however, is distinct from that of everyday life both in its kind and in its direction.

Normal will "streams out" from the "I" and dips into the desire, into the bodily movement, into the action. A will moving in this direction is ineffectual for the awakening of the soul out of ordinary consciousness. But there is another direction for the will that is, in a certain sense, just the opposite. This is the will that is active when, without immediate regard for any external event, one tries to direct one's own "I." This will is active in the efforts one makes to shape one's thinking into a consistent form, to perfect one's feeling, and to follow all impulses of self-development.

---

1. Steiner, *Vom Menschenrätsel (Riddle of Man)*, fourth German edition, p. 161.
2. Kühlewind, "The Two Stages of Consciousness in The Philosophy of Freedom," in *Stages of Consciousness: Meditations on the Boundaries of the Soul* (Great Barrington, MA: Lindisfarne Press, 1984).

In a general increase of the forces of will in this direction there lies what one needs to awaken from everyday consciousness. It is particularly helpful, in the pursuit of this goal, to look at the life of nature with an inward, feeling participation. One attempts, for example, to look at a plant in such a way that one does not merely take in its form in thoughts, but also to some extent one *feels together with* the inner life that stretches itself forth in the stem, unfolds in the leaves' width, opens the inner to the outer in the blossom, and so on. In this kind of thinking, will resonates, too, as a will developed in devotion that guides the soul. It does not take its start from the soul, but directs its effect upon the soul. Of course, at first one may believe that this will has its origin in the soul. In the experience of the process itself, however, one notices that through this reversal of the will the soul has grasped something spiritual that is external to the soul.

"If the will has been strengthened in this direction, and if the *life* of thought has been grasped in the manner indicated, then a different consciousness sets itself off from normal consciousness. This *other* consciousness relates to normal consciousness as the latter relates to the weaving of dream images. And this kind of *seeing awareness* is in a position to know the spiritual world experientially."[3]

In the observation of nature (depending on the intensity of the attention) the direction of will called for here is realized: *a receptive* will, which meets the equally will-filled cosmic ideas for which natural phenomena are the *signs*.[4] It is as if our human will

---

3. Steiner, *Vom Menschenraetsel*, p. 163ff.
4. Steiner, *The Archangel Michael*, Nov. 30, 1919 (from CW 194); *The World of the Senses and the World of the Spirit*, Dec. 28, 1911 (CW 134); *Allgemeine Menschenkunde als Grundlage der Pädagogik*, Aug. 23, 27, 1919 (CW 293).

were to say, "Thy will be done." It is a *spontaneous* will, as paradoxical as the expression may sound. We find this kind of spontaneous will in every artistic activity and in children's play. It is not by accident that we call music-making, for example, *"playing music."* In childhood, the organs of speech, with supraconscious genius, "learn" intuitively that they can spontaneously follow the intention to speak. This is just what the organs for an artistic activity (the hands, for example) must achieve through practice, to be able to follow artistic inspiration through a similarly spontaneous will. This will is at one with what could be called the spontaneous attention, which is carried along by, and allows itself to be imprinted by, the *streaming* element that is always present in art. In every art, it is the discovery of this streaming element that makes the activity possible—even the passive reception of an artwork.

In perceiving, in art, and also in the practice and reception of religious rites, the normal will of attention is altered through its encounter with higher and more powerful "idealities": higher and more powerful, that is, than those with which everyday consciousness works. In the schooling of consciousness, and particularly in the beginning, the greatest difficulty lies in finding this paradoxical will, since initially there are no higher idealities in sight. Meditative themes *become* such idealities when they reveal their "meaning" to the meditating attentiveness. For this, concentratedness, which is precisely the reversed gesture of the will, is helpful and is in fact a precondition.

This concentrated attentiveness is developed through prior exercises such as, for example, the "control of thought" which takes as its theme a simple, fabricated object: its mental picture, thoughts about it, and finally its functional idea.[5] The fundamental obstacle to entry into the path of schooling is presented by the task of finding the "spontaneous" receptive will, the "streaming" element that helps to carry and sustain attention, within *this* exercise. For without this "reversed" will, it is hard to find our way to the relaxed, uncramped and yet concentrated attentiveness—a kind of "active relaxation."[6] It is also difficult because, in the schooling of consciousness, attention has nothing *else* to occupy it: there are no fingers to move, no brush to guide, and so forth.

The reversal of the attentiveness-will always comes about in these cases at a point where the subject meets an intersubjective, universal sphere: the Logos. It may be the language of music, the language of Shakespeare, of nature, or of a ritual. Wherever the life of human ideas touches on greater ideas, attentiveness becomes receptive; it allows itself to be taught afresh, just as it was taught in childhood during the acquisition of speech. Through the word heard, and its understanding, it became *intentional* (that is, *conceptual*) attentiveness, and always directed toward a conceptual "something"—toward the crystallization points of conceptualities offered through language. In this sphere of consciousness, word (to the extent that the word signifies something perceptual), concept, and thing are still one. In the Consciousness Soul,[7] however, in which thinking has become independent of language, the natural object (not understood inwardly or functionally) becomes alienated from thinking. We recognize it by its external characteristics. This same stance within consciousness has spread to all

---

5. Kühlewind, "On the Experience of Concepts," in *Goetheanum*, no. 38, 1985. For control of thoughts, see exercises 1, 2, 3 and 7 in the present volume.

6. Aldous Huxley, *The Art of Seeing*, Berkeley, CA: Creative Arts, 1982.

7. Kühlewind, *Das Licht des Wortes*, chapter 1.

that is fabricated, although *its* functional idea is quite accessible to human beings.[8]

In the "control of thoughts,"[9] there first come tentative sequences of thought and mental pictures that circle around the form, characteristics, production of the object, and so forth. Next, the experience of the *function*, and so of the idea of the thing comes to the fore—the idea without which it would not be *that* thing, and without which we would not know how it functions. If we as practitioners do not perceive this possibility within thinking for ourselves, then it is to be recommended. For with the dawning of the *idea-character* of the object, significant changes occur within the practice of the exercise.[10] It is fruitful, from the beginning, not to picture or think of the object as static, but as functioning, to become aware of its word-character.

This heals our conceptual life. Its nominalism (thinking a thing according to its external characteristics) is conquered by the re-intuiting of the functional idea.

Human-made objects are experienced in their dignity. They are, after all, a new creation on earth through humankind. This dignity and meaning, new even for the angels, is described by Rilke in his *Duino Elegies*:

> Are we *here*, perhaps, to say, "House,
> Bridge, Well, Gate, Cup, Fruit-tree, Window"—
> At the highest, "Pillar, Tower..."?
>
> (IX Elegy)

---

8. Steiner, "On Some Results of Initiation," in *How to Know Higher Worlds* (CW 10); also *An Outline of Esoteric Science* (CW 13).

9. On "control of thoughts," see exercises 1, 2, 3 and 7 in the present volume.

10. Steiner, *Guidance in Esoteric Training*, London: Rudolf Steiner Press, 1998 (CW 42), chapter 1.

And the stars higher. New ones. The stars of the land of suffering.
The Lament names them slowly: "Here,
look: the 'Knight,' the 'Staff,' and the fuller constellation
they call 'Garland of Fruit.' Then, further toward the Pole:
'Cradle,' 'Path,' 'The Burning Bush,' 'Puppet,' 'Window.'

(X Elegy)

The Logos-Sphere is touched on at its lowest level. With this, consciousness meets an element superior to it, as in art, to the extent that the word-likeness of the ideas and their understanding flashes forth in the exercise as an experience. Attention can undergo a metamorphosis at this point, turn around, and become *receptive*. It can experience that, though the mental picture and the thinking of an object consist of attention itself, it can produce them through the grace of the Logos, which is active in the middle of the soul. Attentiveness returns to the streaming element of the Logos sphere—from which it was born.

With this, the practitioner discovers a higher being, a higher sense of "I," within his or her own soul. For wherever a word or the word-like is to be experienced, it must have a source, and this can only be an I-being. It is the encounter with the higher "I" in this experience, through this unassuming exercise, the source of the new feeling, that is called "certainty and security." It comes from the experience of I AM, of one's own spiritual being, which needs no "proofs" or supports. At the same time, the dread of this encounter is the greatest obstacle to "letting attentiveness go," so that it can become like an artistic gesture and yet (in contrast to artistic activity) remain in the nonperceptual. It becomes clear what an inestimable aid art offers to the practitioner, and also where the limits to this aid lie, and why, therefore, art cannot replace cognitive schooling. Art has other goals, which must remain within the perceptual realm.

The presence of a universal within the soul—the presence of the Logos—is suggested in the famous fragment of Heraclitus: "The soul has a Logos that grows by itself." In the addition to Chapter X of the *Philosophy of Freedom*, there is a description of the inherent "contradiction" in the human being: to be able to draw individual intuitions from out of the universal element of ideas.

For meditation, attention must already be strong enough to approach the theme (which is initially understood only as a sound) with an expectant attitude: essentially empty, yet self-contained. Attention must be already reversed, already receptive, awaiting the Higher, free from all mental pictures of what the Higher might be—mental pictures which could only be obstacles to encountering it. For this, attention has to have become as supple and selfless as the pianist's fingers, which are guided by musical intuition and yet remain "fluid,"—as the attention is guided by meditative intuition. The experience of the life within consciousness, of the living Word, is described by Paul in the Epistle to the Galatians (2:20): "Not I live, but Christ lives in me."

The human soul grows stronger through its encounter with the Higher, so that it can take a further step upward on the heavenly stair. The encounter is often painful, and sometimes extinguishes the consciousness, the "seeing," of the poet. It often happened in this way to Dante (*Paradiso* XIV.76, XXIII.35, XXV.121, XXXIII.76), but the same greater Light again and again gave him new, higher powers of sight. Beatrice explained to him,

> Love, which pacifies this Heaven,
> Welcomes you in with gentle virtue,
> To prepare the candle for its flame.
> (XXX.62–64)

The meeting is often portrayed as a battle (Genesis 32:24–29) in which the human will, the word-oriented attentiveness, is "reversed," and gains (fights for) a new form and name from above. The essence of such a battle is represented by Rilke in his poem, "The Seer":

> Whomever this Angel overcame
> (The Angel that so often renounces battle),
> *He* goes forth upright and straight, and great,
> From out of that hard hand
> That molded itself to him as if it formed him.
> Victory no longer interests him.
> His growth is: to be deeply conquered
> By what is ever greater—and greater.
>
> GEORG KÜHLEWIND,
> (from "The Reversal of the Will,"
> in *Goetheanum*, Feb. 9, 1986.)

ART AND KNOWLEDGE

ON THEIR MEDITATIVE SOURCE

These two spiritual phenomena seem at first easy to distinguish: knowing or cognition (knowledge) occurs in the inner space of the soul and the spirit; art always has to enter into the perceptual world and therefore the form in which it appears always has to do with materiality. The "appearance" of cognition or its fruits generally has no aesthetic pretensions. What has been cognized or known need not even be expressed. Its form of appearance is in any case secondary, and takes place *after* cognition. In art, appearance is of the essence; there is nothing *before* its appearance. This appearance may first occur in the imagination—as an image, as poetry or as music—but then it is furnished with its "sensory-material garment."

In this regard, art shows itself analogous to language, which also has its two sides. The inner side is the meaning, the sense, which then appears outwardly as an acoustic or visual phenomenon. Only the "inner" side of an artistic phenomenon is not (merely) thought; otherwise art would be superfluous.

What is *common* to both art and to cognition is creativity: both produce something new. We can guess at their common root. We need to investigate what it gives rise to.[1]

We can thank their common source that in both of these spiritual phenomena meaning, sense, and saying come to light—in a

---

1. Learning and practicing art brings with it many understandings, but its goal is not to be found in these, but in the meaningful alteration of the sensory world.

word: what is logos-like or idea-like; that is, something that *speaks*. But what art says cannot be put into in words. A good poem, for example, cannot be rendered by other words. Art is received through feeling. Feeling is to be found behind every artistic fantasy. And therefore an artistic phenomenon, if it can be replaced by thoughts or by a conceptual explanation, is not art.[2] For art speaks to the "childlike" human being, who receives the world in a feeling/willing or willing/feeling way, with a reversed will that is imprinted by the object.

"CHILDLIKENESS" OF THE IDEA-FEELING

Nature and the divine/spiritual world (which today we call the inner source from which everything new comes) speak through a kind of originally unseparated feeling/willing. They do so in a kind of archaic, participatory consciousness that is repeated today by the small child in a somewhat changed form. This is the kind of feeling that oriented archaic human beings in nature in their technological achievements (building, ceramics, and so on) and in the rituals and religious practices that extend beyond biological necessity. Such archaic perception was a *full* perceiving of things, in which, rather than arriving at ideality along a separate path, through thinking or its precursors, the ideality of what was perceived was included in perceiving itself. The inner space in which thinking can live independently of perceiving only built itself up later through word-concepts, concepts given by language—such

---

2. Many artistic practices today imagine they can do without beauty. They produce "interesting," "unusual," and "stimulating" objects of art. Mostly they require conceptual explanation and also stimulate it. It is at least questionable whether there isn't a misunderstanding here about the category of "art."

as, for example, conjunctions—that do not correspond to any sensory perception. Self-consciousness comes once thinking has already separated itself from cognitive feeling and willing and formed for itself a structure capable of reflection. Such consciousness is largely on the level of the past—of the previously thought, the already-imagined, and so forth—but it can touch the level of presence-of-mind, of truth, of living thinking (imagination) in each new understanding.[3]

Today, children in their early years are still *wholly* organs of the senses, and this global sensing consciousness consists precisely of feeling oriented toward the outside. The individual regions of sensation—which sustain the different senses through language and children's human surroundings, and which are completely separated for adults because of "education"—differentiate out of this.[4] Still, it is well known that sensory perception remains permeated by feeling for children until everyday concepts "dry out" the feelings from the perceptions.

In art, we return to cognitive or communicative feelings that may be compared with the universally communicative element of thinking that we hold in common. Thinking here is not yet separate from feeling but, so to say, held in suspension within the feeling that intelligently appreciates art.

Ideas that are *felt* are still more open, more "generous," than living ideas. This is why a landscape can be painted "beautifully" in more than one way, and a piece of music can be played "beautifully" in various ways. "Beauty," like the True and the Good, is an

3. Kühlewind, *Das Licht des Wortes* (The Light of the Word), chapter 1, "The life of the consciousness soul," Stuttgart, 1984.
4. Kühlewind, *Die Belehrung der Sinne* (The Schooling of the Senses), chapter 2, "Language and Senses," Stuttgart, 1990.

intuition or experience that can no more be founded on the level of past thinking (or discursive thinking) than the other two fundamental ideas—or fundamental ideas in general.

Because art speaks from and to feeling, there is "regressiveness" within it, a return to "childlikeness," since its activity or reception never involves only one sense, but in practice *all* of our senses. This is why, in contemplating art, we can speak of "balance," "movement," "warm feelings," "hard tones," and so on. In art, we can still perceive in a childlike/feeling way, but this only refers to one quality of artistic consciousness. The "contents" of art, that is, its specific feeling-qualities, are not at all childlike.

HOW TO BEAR IDEAS

If we compare art and nature, both are sensory experiences. Both radiate feeling and willing, and indeed consist of these elements. However, art is like a piece of nature touched by human beings, tamed, brought close.

> For the beautiful is nothing but
> the beginning of the terrifying, which we can still barely tolerate
> and we marvel at it so much, because it calmly distains
> to destroy us.

This is how Rilke summarizes his aesthetics in the first of the *Duino Elegies*. In the second Elegy he adds,

> Where are the days of Tobias,
> when one of those most radiant ones stood at the door,
> disguised a bit for travel and no longer frightening.

As the archangel is "disguised a bit," making himself bearable for the human being's sake, so is nature in art. The elements of language, sounds, grammar, syntax, do not come from nature—neither do the elements of art. There are no pure musical tones in nature, not even among birds; there are no color combinations of the kind you find in a painted picture. Not even naturalism has achieved this; and wherever it does seem to succeed the question arises as to whether it is really art or some kind of imitation of nature. No entity in nature can be seen as we see a statue: still and moving simultaneously.

Art is not a given for human beings: it is our creation. We create new feelings through art, new formations in feeling. The artist is inspired by a new feeling and gives it expression in the perceptual world ("and" is a conjunction here meaning something like, "at the same time"). We could say that natural objects arise when a higher will moves into sense-perceptible materiality. Art arises when a human will, led by feeling-inspiration, acts intelligently in materiality. Through dead concepts, we fight off the mighty ideas to which we are exposed in the contemplation of nature. We cannot bear their vastness. Dead concepts are poured quickly over perception and neutralize or kill what streams toward us from nature.

GENESIS OF THE IDEA

In every idea, in every thought, we can discover a *will*—it *wills* to become this idea. When a new idea is on the way, this will that appears first and produces it—like a crinkling, a gentle fold in the blue heaven of heightened awareness. Out of it a *feeling* forms that is a little more contoured than the billow of the will. And out of the feeling pours a *living stream of thought*, which is already more distinct, but is still without language or words. It is the waters of this stream that then crystallize into more or less fixed thoughts that condense into words—which say something only to the hearer or receiver who re-awakens them to life.

The genesis of an *artistic idea* runs a similar course. The first two stages are the same. After the cloud of feeling has formed, however, the sensorially perceptible development of the artistic phenomenon occurs immediately. Living thinking and the level of past thoughts are completely avoided. If an idea has concretized itself to the point of living thinking, which can be expressed many different ways, then no true, good artwork can come of it. To be true and good, it would have had to stay in feeling (in "objective" feeling). Art always brings forth a feeling form into the world of sensory perceptions: a form whose original essence addresses itself to feeling and to receptive will.

MEDITATION AS RESEARCH

Some decades before our time, science and art lived out of a more or less superconscious connection with the sources of ideas, including artistic ideas. These connections, like everything given or gifted to us, continually threaten to grow thinner and even to disappear completely. Science today has come to the point where it no longer attains the reality of nature and the human being. For both reasons, it is appropriate to our time to engage in meditative practice.[5]

Such practice would consist in human beings trying, through exercises of consciousness, to extend the point- or lightening-like connection with the level of understanding or presence-of-mind

---

5. Kühlewind, *From Normal to Healthy,* chapter 5, Great Barrington, MA: Anthroposophic Press, 1995. See also "Schulung der Aufmerksamkeit" (Schooling of Attention) in *Freiheit Erüben* (Practicing Freedom), Stuttgart, 1988; and *Die Belehrung der Sinne* (Schooling of the Senses), chapter 8, "Exercises of Perception," Stuttgart, 1990.

that we touch on in every new moment of understanding. Then, it involves learning to articulate oneself within higher levels (practicing a wordless thinking and perception) to strengthen and intensify the connection. Later, we can then extend this connection to higher levels of consciousness like cognitive feeling (which are normally superconscious for us).

The path of research-meditation begins with bringing the theme—the research question or problem—into a form suitable for meditation. This form can be a sentence or an image, or, for more advanced and practiced researchers it may be a situation or question that is barely formulated, or not formulated at all, a simple "How is that?" or even just a "How?" The researcher concentrates on the theme (on the wordless meaning of the sentence, or on the question in a picture-form) until the theme becomes transparent, and attention has moved over into a receptive gesture. The theme then dissolves into a living thinking, which in turn is always accompanied by a feeling.

The next step consists in the researcher "renouncing" the first stage, that of the clearly worked out flowing, living element of thinking, by allowing this element to become transparent and then shifting the attention to feeling. If you can consciously move within the feeling of the theme, as previously in the transition to living thinking, then you may work out, within feeling, a *feeling form*—which is cloud-like, but still has its specific character as feeling. This happens through an attention that *feels*, not thinks, not perceives.

The next stage adds another renunciation to what has already been attained, to the feeling-form. Through concentration in feeling, the form of feeling can change again. We can say that the feeling pales, but at the same time becomes a willing, and there now rises into awareness (which itself has changed from a feeling to a willing attention) a still more general formation, a "more indeterminate" one in the normal sense, but quite specific in a higher sense, a *form of will*, in fact. We can think here of the single moral intuition of the New Testament, "Love one another as I have loved you." It is an intuition on the level of the will. To realize it on earth we have to transform it (always through new intuitions in feeling and living thinking) all the way into everyday consciousness, so that it becomes effective in particular cases.

This bringing things down to earth is just as hard to learn as rising up. In rising, we encounter something new on each level attained, and the experience on the higher level does not simply "correspond" to what we have experienced on a lower level, but always adds something new to it. If we want to "draw down" a cognition at the level of will, we must above all be careful not to bring it too quickly, out of impatience, to the level of a text. This can distort its meaning or lose it entirely. We are to seek patiently for the new feeling, from which the stream of thinking then flows forth, and finally we allow the formulation to inspire us with a meditative text through new feeling-linguistic intuitions. Spiritual experiences can only be given a remotely adequate expression through symbolic language (texts, image, action).

In our day, the capacities we brought with us or developed unconsciously fade away by about the middle of our life. It is therefore appropriate to undertake a schooling of consciousness. Whether we have to do then with an act of meditative cognition, of research, or of *artistic inspiration*, the path upward is the same. In both cases, the meditant needs to feel an anticipatory relationship with the theme. The way downward, however, becomes different at the level of cognitive feeling. In artistic meditation, the very next step would be to take action. Feeling inspiration must not shift downward into the stream of thinking, but should grasp and direct an intelligent, artistic will.

ARTISTIC ACTIVITY FROM WILL AND FEELING THAT SEE

Every artistic education therefore has two goals. On the one hand, the specific feeling sensitivity for the perceptual field of the art form in question has to be developed. On the other hand, through the engagement with the materiality in question (the instrument, the brush and paint, clay and stone, one's own body, and so on) the specific "technique" of the art also has to be developed so that, for example, the hand and through it the whole body, become a *speech organ*, and can follow the guiding inspiration and implant it, in its feeling-form, into the sensory world. This requires the development of an intelligent, "seeing" will, which is not given its goals, its forms of movement, by thinking or by mental picturing, but which carries the "what" of the will *within itself*. Actually, artistic "technique" always means this kind of creation through the "seeing" will in the given perceptual field of that art form.[6]

This requires a twofold preparation: knowledge of the material (instrument, color, clay) and the connection with the guiding sense (sight for painting, hearing for music, seeing/touching for

---

6. When we speak, we do not prescribe movements to our speech organs by means of mental images or by thinking, nor could we. Nor do we worry what the speech organs are doing. This is not simply the result of habituation, since small children do not know what they have to do with their speech organs to reproduce what they have heard. We aim, in artistic education, at a similar superconscious activity of the will.

sculpture, and so on). It is through the latter that artistic creation operates actively and passively at the same time, prescribes form and perceives it—as, in speaking, activity and passivity (articulation and reception of what is produced) coincide.

Familiarity with the material aspect consists basically in a growing-together of the sensory organism, especially that of the sense that guides the art form in question, with the instrument (in many arts, the instrument is one's own body). This means that the sense of touch and movement, accompanied or guided by feeling, extends onto the instrument. Then we "feel" the whole mechanism of the piano, of the brush, of the paint, of the bow's sliding over the strings, etc.). The instrument itself becomes a sense organ and a limb. Artistic activity, together with the instrument, becomes *permeated with feeling.* Only this can assure artistic quality, *so that you can say something with it.*[7]

In cognitive meditation, cognition concretizes itself in its descent through the step from living thinking to formulated thoughts. This corresponds, in art, to the transition from the feeling form to the perceptual world. The perception that arises remains ambiguous, like a meditative text. The way from feeling onward passes through the guiding sense (though all the other senses resonate along with it), and through this there arises, out of the feeling form, the "image" that is to appear (including an "auditory image"), that later (or, as in the theater, at the same moment) affects the audience by a reversed pathway. Namely, through the guiding sense, in which the others resonate alongside, the perceptual picture is received, and through

---

7. To make poems and write artistic prose means working with the qualities of sound or their mental pictures. The silent reading of artistic texts requires at least a mental picture of the way they sound (until the fourth century C.E., everyone read out loud).

the variegated sensory activity feeling comes into resonance and becomes formed accordingly.

FEELABLE THEMES

In former artistic eras, the themes were feelable. Therefore they could inspire artistic activity. The Madonna and child could ignite religious feeling, at least for certain intense moments, and offer to the picture, to the painter, a kind of basis in feeling. The same could be said of a landscape or a face. As perception, imagery, and even religious life began to lose the quality of feeling—the feeling element—such themes became increasingly pretexts to use elements (sensory qualities) that still contained feeling and could arouse it. The theme itself, however, no longer inspired any feeling.

In contemporary art the pretext is dropped and work goes forward with the elements, the component means of the kind of art being practiced. This is least successful in arts that use language as their element. There, the interweaving of the "theme" with its form of expression is the strongest of all. On the other hand, the theme can be handled and understood at many levels due to the vertical multiplicity of the words' meanings.[8]

Through the theme (the picture image) the observer of fine arts can easily be misled. For he or she can turn toward the work of art with intentional attention (oriented toward something known, something given in advance)—as suggested during many art-gallery tours. "Here you see two cows, a windmill, a farmer at the

---

8. Vertical ambiguity of the verbal concepts given by language is easiest to experience in the symbolic language of myths and fairy tales. An object or being means, in its pictorial quality, much that cannot be expressed any other way. This quality of words is made use of in demanding texts of all kinds, including meditative texts.

plough," or some such. In modern, non-figurative art, we find no "thing," only two-dimensional flecks of color that of themselves do not make a work of art. So the observer is (almost) forced to activate a receptive (meditative) attention; it is only through this that he or she could receive the feeling-message of the pictures (basically the same situation applies to a figurative image).[9]

THE MEANING OF ART

Through art, the sense-perceptible world is changed. Knowledge changes nothing about the world—only applied knowledge would do so. We can apply our cognitions in a meaning-creating way or a meaning-less way. The latter takes place in all transformations of the perceptual world that occur out of egoism, including those that encompass all of humanity. This includes all technological arrangements that serve egoism, comfort, secondary human instincts, and that do not "speak," do not "communicate" anything.

It is through human beings that meaning-lessness comes into the world. Of course, what has arisen meaninglessly can later be given meaning by placing it in the service of a meaningful, meaning-creating life. Art changes the perceptual world "in a speaking way," by creating new meanings. In this sense, it is the sequel to the old, sacred way of life, in which *everything* was meaningful—and perhaps it is the prelude to a new human epoch, in which the human being will give existence a new meaning.

---

9. Both styles of attention are well known to us. One happens during eye-contact (a receptive, inviting gaze); the other in the ophthamologist's look, which is directed, intentional observation.

Bibliography

Georgiades, Thrasybulos. *Nennen und Erklingen: Die Zeit als Logos* ("Naming and Speaking: The Time as Logos"). Geottingen: Vanderhoek and Ruprecht, 1985.

Huxley, Aldous. *The Art of Seeing.* New York and London: Harper, 1942.

Kühlewind, Georg. *Aufmerksamkeit und Hingabe.* Stuttgart: Freies Geistesleben, 1988.

———. *Die Belehrung der Sinne. Wege zur fühlenden Wahrnehmung.* Stuttgart: Freie Geistesleben, 1998.

———. *Die Diener des Logos.* Stuttgart: Freies Geistesleben, 1981.

———. *Die Esoterik des Erkennens und Handelns: in der Philosophie der Freiheit und der Geheimwissenschaft Rudolf Steiners.* Stuttgart: Freies Geistesleben, 1995.

———. *From Normal to Healthy: Paths to the Liberation of Consciousness.* Trans. M. Lipson. Hudson, NY: Lindisfarne Press, 1994.

———. *Das Licht des Wortes.* Stuttgart: Freies Geistesleben, 1984.

———. *The Life of the Soul between Subconscious and Supraconscious.* Tans. M. Lipson. Hudson, NY: Lindisfarne Press, 1990.

———. *The Light of the "I": Guidelines for Meditation.* Great Barrington, MA: Lindisfarne Books, 2008.

———. *Meditationen: Über Zen-Buddhismus, Thomas von Aquin und Anthroposophie.* Stuttgart: Freies Geistesleben, 2008.

———. "On the Experience of Concepts." In *Goetheanum*, No. 38. 1985.

———. "The Perception of Spatial and Temporal Forms," in *Goetheanum.* May 20, 1984.

———. "The Purity of Striving." "The Second Level of Meditation." In *Die Wahrheit Tun.* Stuttgart: Freies Geistesleben, 1978.

———. "The Reversal of the Will." In *Goetheanum.* February 9, 1986.

———. "The Schooling of Attention." In *Practicing Freedom.* Fair Oaks, CA: Rudolf Steiner College Press, 1988.

———. *Der Sprechende Mensch.* Stuttgart: Freies Geistesleben, 1995.

————. *Stages of Consciousness: Meditations on the Boundaries of the Soul.* Trans. M. St. Goar. Hudson, NY: Lindisfarne Press, 1984. "The Two Levels of Consciousness in *The Philosophy of Freedom*.".

Steiner, Rudolf. *Allgemeine Menschenkunde als Grundlage der Pädagogik* (Aug. 23 and 27, 1919). Published in English as *The Foundations of Human Experience*. Hudson, NY: Anthroposophic Press, 1996 (also *The Study of Man*).

————. *Founding a Science of the Spirit.* Revised trans. M. Barton. London: Rudolf Steiner Press, 1999.

————. *Guidance in Esoteric Training: From the Esoteric School.* Revised trans. O. Barfield and C. Davey. London: Rudolf Steiner Press, 2001.

————. *How to Know Higher Worlds: A Modern Path of Initiation.* Trans. C. Bamford. Hudson, NY: SteinerBooks, 1994.

————. "The Mission of the Archangel Michael" (lecture 6, November 30, 1919). In *The Archangel Michael: His Mission and Ours,* Hudson, NY: Anthroposophic Press, 1994.

————. *An Outline of Esoteric Science.* Trans. C. E. Creeger. Great Barrington, MA: SteinerBooks, 1997 (previous trans., *An Outline of Occult Science*).

————. *The Riddle of Humanity.* Trans. J. F. Logan (lectures 7, 14, August 12 and September 2, 1916), London: Rudolf Steiner Press, 1990.

————. *The Riddle of Man: From the Thinking, Observations, and Contemplations of a Series of German and Austrian Personalities: What They Have Said and Left Unsaid.* Trans. W. Lindeman, Spring Valley, NY: Mercury Press, 1990 (*Vom Menschenrätsel,* fourth German edition. Dornach, Switzerland: Rudolf Steiner Nachlassverwaltung, 1957).

————. "The Threshold of the Spiritual World." In *A Way of Self Knowledge and The Threshold of the Spiritual World.* Trans. C. Bamford. Great Barrington, MA: SteinerBooks, 2006.

————. *The World of the Senses and the World of the Spirit.* Trans. n/a. N. Vancouver: Steiner Book Centre, 1979 (lecture 2, December 28, 1911).

Breinigsville, PA USA
24 March 2011
258334BV00001B/1/P